Life, Death and all the Diabetes In Between

Published in Canada by

Life Rattle Press

Toronto, Ontario, Canada

Life Rattle Press New Writers Series

ISSN 1713 8981

ISBN: 978-1-989861-33-2

© 2021 by Abdullah Sher

All rights reserved. No part of this book may be reproduced in any form or by any means, electronic or mechanical, including photocopying, recording, or by any information storage and retrieval system, without permission in writing from the publisher or the author.

Cover design by Hafsa Siddiqui

Copyedited by John Dunford

Typeset by Abdullah Sher

To diabetics who feel alone.

To diabetics who go low after a swim.

To diabetics who've suffered from seizures.

To diabetics who've collapsed into comas.

To diabetics who survived until insulin was discovered but died before their first dose.

To diabetics who despise their disease.

To diabetics who've accepted it.

To diabetics who sing "Country Roads" in September because it's no longer summer.

To the Camp Huronda August 2017 LDPs.

To Benji's broken hammock.

To anyone ever affected by diabetes: I hope you enjoy these stories

Contents

1. Dada..1
2. The Half-Car..9
3. Mackenzie and Squirtle...15
4. Diagnosed..21
5. Diabetes: A Death Sentence..27
6. Rice Pudding..35
7. High and Lows..45
8. The Bloody Problem with Glucose Testing............................51
9. CGMs: Video Recorders Not Snapshot Cameras...................59
10. Aging Ears and Aging Years...67
11. Walker...73
12. Gratitude..79
13. Half-Drowned..89

14. Rage Room 97

15. Time To Go 103

16. God WIlling 109

17. Transient Means Fleeting 117

18. Second Family 123

19. The Gila Monster: A Venemous Miracle 129

20. GLP-1 RAs: From Injectable to SNACable 137

21. Inverse Vaccines: Immune System Re-Education 145

22. Aceruloplasminemia and Diabetes Mellitus 153

23. Outsider Once Again 161

24. Runaway Boy 167

25. Attention 179

26. Miscellaneous Problems of the Food Kind 187

27. Broken Bones and Stitches 197

28. Alex 205

Chapter 1
Dada

"Sudeer!" Dada yells from his room. I make my way to the open door and see my grandfather sitting at his study table with his cane leaning by his side. "Is Haroon back from work? And have you called Rabia yet?"

No, Baba isn't back from work yet. No, the head servant, Sudeer, hasn't called Mama to ask if she is on her way home from college. Not that it stops Dada from asking about them every few hours.

Just a regular day in the Sher household.

We live comfortably on the main floor of a house with my two grandparents, my two cousins and their parents, my parents, me and my soon-to-be baby brother. A family rents out the second floor. A slide and a swing set stand in the huge front yard. Dada purchased the twenty-year-old house when he returned to Pakistan from Saudi Arabia years ago, back when there was no difference between house and mansion. He's micromanaged and renovated the property multiple times ever since.

Most mornings, the men go to work, Mama goes to college and my aunt goes shopping with my younger cousin, Ali, after dropping off Ahmed, my older cousin, at kindergarten. I'm left at home for most of the day—just me, Dada, my grandmother Dadi and the servants.

Not that I mind.

I play with a toy train in my Scooby-Doo T-shirt on Dada's bed right next to his desk. I start school in September. It's still six months away, but it is school, and if crying in daycare taught me anything, it's that the swings and slides at the school bore me compared to the newer, better ones on our lawn. And that Mama won't be there—and if she isn't there, and if Dada and Dadi aren't there either, it's gonna suck.

"Abu-ji!" Sudeer shouts and barges into Dada's room. "There's a man from the Al-Jannat Clinic on the landline."

Al-Jannat, a charity clinic for the poor that Dada opened since forever ago and named it after his mother, charges deeply reduced fees for health tests and minor surgeries. Dada doesn't work anymore, but the people he trusts to run it, always find problems to complain about.

"Alright, sir," Dada says when he picks up the phone. "What seems to be the problem this time?"

My grandfather sinks back into his chair and grabs a cookie from one of the many sweet-filled steel milk jars stored below his desk. He tilts his head, nestling the phone between his head and shoulder, and now hands-free he positions his left hand like a plate and munches on the cookie with his right.

Crunch! Crunch!

Despite his best efforts, cookie crumbs slide onto Dada's white beard. He glances my way, pulls out another cookie and holds his hand out. I snatch the cookie. He smiles.

"Abu-ji!" Sudeer runs into the room again. "The construction workers outside, they uhm, they seem to be packing up for the day…"

Dada frowns. "I'm going to have to call you later," he says into the phone. "No, I did not agree to that. Yes, this conversation will continue later. Good day, sir."

Dada grasps his cane, eases himself up out of his seat and puts on a pair of slippers.

"Alright, I suppose I can pay them a surprise visit." He looks over at me. "Abdullah, would you like to come?"

He extends his old, wrinkled hand.

"Okay, Dada!"

I jump off his bed, reach up and grab his hand. Exiting the house through the kitchen entrance, Dada quickens his pace. I waddle along with a cookie in hand trying to keep up. We turn the corner and enter my parents' room. Part of the wall at the far end lies empty, the bricks scattered around haphazardly. Four men sit around on the ground, cigarettes in hand, the Cokes Dada sent for them half-finished and their tools packed in their boxes.

"*Janaab* (Gentlemen)." Dada's booming voice ends their laughter. He rests his hands lightly on his cane, his face serious and severe. The four men freeze and then look up at Dada.

"S-sir!" stutters one builder. "We were just taking a small brea—"

"And your tools are packed for what reason, then?" Dada says.

The construction worker's shoulders slump.

"Please give us one more chance, sir?" he says with hands clasped.

"You have until the end of the day to finish building this closet—otherwise no pay!" Dada responds.

Dada spots two steel white chairs a few metres away from us.

"You!" he says and points his cane to another worker. "Bring those two chairs. I intend to watch this from start to finish! No corners will be cut. Do I make myself clear?"

The four men restrain a sigh and force out a strained, "Yes, sir!"

I keep eating my cookie.

Later at night I enter Dada and Dadi's room with a picture book in hand. There's plenty of space in my parents' room, even an attached computer room along with my own mini-bed. I just like Dada's room better. A glass table stands beside their bed neatly cluttered with pens and notebooks including the contract with the workers to build the closet in my parents' room. They finally finished it today.

Boxes of pills and needles also occupy the glass table. Every night, Dada takes a lot of pills. And an injection. I'm surprised he doesn't shudder in fear and scream in pain like me when I get my yearly shots. I overheard Baba says it's to control some disease called "sugar." I don't understand how sugar could ever be bad for you.

Dada lies comfortably on his bed as Dadi sleeps beside him. Pillows prop his head. He has all his hair, which always seems more like silk than hair. No one else's hair can compare. Not my Baba's, nor my Mama's, not even my *phuppa's* (uncles's) or my *phuppoe's* (aunt's). Old brown glasses frame Dada's face. His newspaper spreads out in front of him in a splatter of Urdu. The fat black television on the cabinet in front of the bed hums through the familiar beat of the Geo News theme song in the background.

I climb onto the bed and narrow myself into a tiny space between my grandparents. Dadi moves slightly further on her side of the bed. Dada silently pulls a pillow into the space where my head will rest next to his. As I lie down beside him, I time my breathing with his—I breathe in when he breathes in, and I breathe out when he breathes out, and not any other way. Dada's breath smells awful. We lie side by side. One reads. The other pretends he can. I drift off to sleep.

In the morning, I lay in bed alone—my grandparents are up hours before me. They used to be doctors, so waking up bright and early is routine.

Bright rays of sun pierce through my eyelids. I shift through the covers. The bed feels warm. I want to sneak in a few more minutes of sleep. The huge TV in the lounge outside buzzes as the servants serve breakfast.

The bed feels…too warm…and wet?

"Abdullah! *Uttow!* (Get up)!" Baba stands on the other side of the bed. His father scrunches up his nose. He carefully lifts the blanket away and inspects it. The smell within the blanket quickly reaches the open air and jolts me out of my sleep-filled haze. A brown, viscous semi-liquid pools around my hips.

Poop. At four years old you'd think I would've gotten used to going to the washroom instead of using a diaper. *Damn it.*

Baba guards the door as I make a beeline to Dada's washroom. The lecture comes after I make it inside and close the door. "This will be THE LAST time this happens. DO. YOU. UNDERSTAND? The next time this happens—"

"Haroon!" the Sher family patriarch interrupts as he walks into the room. He still wears his slippers and pyjamas and quietly makes his way towards us with his cane. His silky white hair shines in the glowing daylight. A protruding stomach betrays his sweet tooth.

Dada steps slowly but steadily, his strides not long but pronounced. He stands in front of Baba, his eyes at my father's neck level, yet Baba seems to shrink nonetheless.

"He's just a boy, lighten up," Dada says.

"But Abu, this isn't the first time he did this and it always causes a mess in your be—"

Dada's face remains blank and calm. He allows his son time to stop. Both hands rest lightly on his cane.

"Okay, Abu."

"Good," Dada says.

Not that I deserve the intervention. Baba's fed up with my incontinence. Rightfully so. So am I. I never soil Dadas bed after that day ever again.

Still.

I'm glad my grandfather is alive.

Chapter 2

The Half-Car

The light no longer shines through the window. The sun set an hour ago. Invisibility claims the moon tonight. My lips scrunch up as Baba tucks me into bed.

"Do I have to go to sleep this early, Baba? I'm not"—I yawn and hope Baba didn't see it—"tired yet."

An eyebrow arches over me. "Alright, then you can help your mama clean the kitchen, dust the dining room and take out the trash while I lie in the lounge." A small grin twitches at the edges of Baba's mouth.

Damn it.

"Alright, fine," I grumble. "I'll go to sleep."

What four-year-old wants to sleep this early, anyway? Nine p.m. and it's my bedtime, but my parents can stay up for another four hours?! I understand Hamza, my one-year-old brother, needs to sleep early, but that's because he's a baby.

I'm three whole years and a month older than him. I should naturally be allowed to stay awake three times longer than him. It makes absolutely, positively, perfect sense! But I am forced to take—yawn—stupid naps. I hate naps. I want to be an adult. Then I can have no bedtime, just like my parents. The summer days in Pakistan are too long to simply sleep through.

"*Shubakhair* (Good night), Abdullah," Baba whispers as he tucks me into his bed and spreads a new handwoven quilt over me. It's not the biggest bed, but it can easily hold my parents, so the bed is huge for just me.

I snuggle into the fresh new quilt and briefly brush against cool metal. The end of the bed, I realize. I shift my body towards the centre. I don't want to fall off the bed. I curl the quilt against me like a cocoon. A real cocoon protects a caterpillar from the elements and gives comfort while it hibernates. My cocoon protects me from the cold air and hugs me while I nap. The cool blanket contrasts with my warmer body. I can feel my eyelids droop.

"Shubakhair, Baba," I reply.

Baba turns off the light and shuts the door behind him on his way out.

Something seems…out of place. It takes me a moment, but as my eyes adjust to the absence of light, I notice the pitch-black darkness. Not an inch of visible light seeps through the large glass windows in my room or from the gap underneath the door—yet I know for a fact that Mama and Baba sit on the other side of the door in the light-filled TV lounge.

The darkness isn't a familiar feeling. My cocoon feels suffocating rather than comfortable now, more like a fly caught powerless in a spider's web than a caterpillar growing into a butterfly.

My eyes dart back and forth wildly. I can't move my head. A soft shrill ringing reaches my ears. I ignore it. I try and move my hands and my feet. Nothing moves. After swinging like a pendulum in my sockets, my eyes finally slow down. In the pitch-black of my vision, splotches of green and blue appear for seconds, disappear, and then reappear, over and over again.

The Half-Car

The shrill ringing intensifies, like an indescribable reverberation—a sound without an identity, a sound that simply is, increasing in intensity, yet anonymous in form, a cacophony sensed through the body rather than the ears.

One second.
Two seconds.
Ten seconds.
Sixty seconds.
Forever.

Amid the chaotic green and blue splotches, a shape starts to form—the front half of a bright baby blue car with a white stripe running down the middle. The round headlights remind me of the kind I saw in Dada's photo album. A vehicle fit for a millionaire.

Except.

The car has no rear half. It sits on two wheels and rotates. It rotates as if on display—for who, I don't know.

It rotates once.
It rotates twice.
Thrice.
Five times.
Ten times.
Forever.

Overwhelming like a tsunami, encircling like a cyclone, overpowering like a lion, it engulfs me whole.

This must be a dream! It can't be real.
No. A nightmare.
I want to wake up.
Yet I can't wake up.

Four years later, I'm eight years old roaming Square One strolling through the mall with my family. Baba has a smile. Mama glances at multiple clothing stores looking to find bargain sales for children's clothes. Hamza, my brother, tired after two hours of running around, sleeps in his stroller. I don't care about the mall. I don't like shopping; It takes too long.

A flash of blue captivates my attention. A single sideward glance freezes my mind.

There in a small store in Square One, half way across the world, as part of a wall decoration, stands a bright baby blue car with a white stripe running down the middle. The round headlights the kind I saw in Dada's photo album. A vehicle fit for a millionaire.

Except.

The car has no rear half.

Chapter 3
Mackenzie and Squirtle

A soft spring breeze blows across the Broadacres Elementary School playground. Students stand scattered around the huge schoolyard. Most second graders play in two sandboxes. A few first graders slip down the slide in the one of them, trying in vain not to get stuck on the cheap plastic construct gripping their skin.

Some fourth graders play basketball near the tetherball poles on the pavement. The poles stand without both ball and chain. Some third-grade girls play hopscotch and scream shrill cheers when a girl overcomes the monumental challenge of jumping on one knee nine consecutive times.

I sit on the edge of one sandbox, facing my friends Mackenzie and Michael. Mackenzie is showing us some strange sand construct.

"See, I shaped the sand here like a turtle shell, and I made a small extension outward for his swirly tale, and for his limbs, I tucked these small bent twigs snugly around his shell," Mackenzie exclaims. "For his face, I smoothed out a semicircle of sand. He has these big round eyes I can't exactly draw out, but these pebbles should do the trick. And, voila! There you have it! One Squirtle Pokémon!"

Mackenzie's blue eyes swell with pride. Sand sprinkles Mackenzie's white shoes as he crouches. Sand cakes his pudgy fingers and darkens his nails. The sand probably got into his shoes too.

I curl my lip down. I discreetly brush away any sand daring to enter my halo of sand-less wood. Michael crinkles his forehead in deep concentration, trying to comprehend the misshapen mass lying before him.

Sand—what an irksome material. Looking down on my friends crouching in the gritty sandbox from my post on the wide, wooden edge of the sandbox, I try to understand why they love the sand so much. Mrs. Brown, my teacher, describes it as "putting yourself in someone else's shoes." Humph, as if I could tolerate Mackenzie's sand-filled shoes.

"Hey, Mackenzie," I blurt out hoping to interrupt a potential monologue. "What's the point of building all of this?"

My brown-haired friend focuses on me, eyebrows scrunched up, deep in thought. "What do you mean?" he asks. "We build stuff cuz it's fun to mess around, to get imaginative, to build whatever you want!"

"Right but, like, in a couple of minutes, classes resume, everyone runs over the sandbox and everything will be destroyed again!"

"Aaaannd? Your point? It doesn't matter, just gotta rebuild it again or make something new next recess! Now, what do you two think of Squirtle?"

How the heck was sand fun? And how exactly did Mackenzie expect an answer? What Squirtle? The misshapen mass of sand, sticks and stones? Maybe I just need to think more clearly.

Mackenzie describes the Squirtle well enough, so it shouldn't be too hard to visualize what the creature actually looks like. I start by focusing on the head. Or what I think is the head…maybe I'm looking at the tail…or a limb? So, the other side is the face? It looks no different from the tail!

"Wow, Mackenzie. I, uh, I couldn't have done a better job myself!" Michael says.

Strange. He usually talks nonstop, faster than the Flash.

"Man, you should, uh, try to make Wartortle or Blastoise next!" Michael cries out.

Apparently he also watches Pokémon. While he kneels in the sandbox to get a better view, I notice small flecks of sand slip into his shoes. I quickly check my surroundings again—my halo of sand-free wood remains intact.

I like the small "woods" right next to the sandbox, full with a few trees, some large slabs of rocks and plenty of flat wood chips. The chips occasionally get into your shoes, but due to their size, removing them is much easier than removing stupid sand.

"Abdullah? You there?"

I blink.

Michael and Mackenzie stare at me.

"Uh..." I scratch the back of my head and smile an awkward smile. I didn't expect to be caught zoning out. "Sorry. What did I miss?"

"What do you think of my Squirtle?" Mackenzie says. "Come down here and get a better look."

Michael keeps himself crouched next to Mackenzie.

"See, I'd rather not step inside the sandbox," I say.

"Why not? It's just sand."

"I don't like sand that much. It gets in your fingers, in your shoes, in your hair if you fall in it and in your butt cheeks if it gets in your pants. Sand feels uncomfortable when it gets in and removing it is even harder sometimes. It just loves to get stuck in every nook and cranny. So, no thank you. I will not step in."

Wow. I surprised myself. I hadn't spoken like that in a long time.

"Well, you still didn't answer my other question. What do you think of my Squirtle?"

The bell rings. I'm saved.

"Aw, man! Now we gotta destroy Squirtle," Mackenzie whines.

I roll my eyes. What did Mackenzie say about the constructs being destroyed? I'm not surprised. Relieved, yes, but surprised, no. The "Squirtle" falls into oblivion in the next few minutes as students trample through the sandbox back to class.

We all go back inside for another regular math class. I check my fingernails and shoes for any stray sand particles, while Michael and Mackenzie furiously clean their hands at the classroom sink before the lesson starts. I stroll back to my desk. They wince back to their seats and then try and discreetly remove sand from their shoes without anyone noticing.

Sand is worthless—it brings nothing but wincing feet, dirty hands and misshapen animals called "Squirtle." Best to stay away from it.

Life remains simple that way.

Chapter 4
Diagnosed

I shift around on the pale white tile floor of the music room. Twenty-five grade four students sit in five equal rows, our bums on the floor, each of us gradually shifting from sitting cross-legged and stretched legs to kneeling in an attempt to remain comfortable as we listen to our music teacher, Mrs. Edmund.

My eyes shift to the clock by the classroom door—3:10. Class ends in twenty minutes. Then Mama will pick me up and we can skedaddle home and I can rush to the washroom. Maybe I'll be able to hold it in…

"Okay class, today we will listen to 'In the Hall of the Mountain King,' and afterwards, I will explain your final assignment of the year. Listen closely," Mrs. Edmund says.

The song starts quietly, with slow bass drums, and then the tempo picks up. The orchestra winds out the climax with a harmonic cacophony of symbols, fast bass drums and a slew of clarinets, flutes and trumpets. To the ear, a loud, yet harmonic, clash of sound—to my bowel, unfortunately, a sign to increase downward movement as well.

I try to clench my buttocks. Damn it, never mind getting home in a few minutes, my bowel is seconds away from ruining me if I don't move *right now!*

"Mrs. Edmund, may I go to the washroom?" I blurt out, my hand shooting up into the air, the other hand propping my body up off the floor. I widen my eyes. My buttocks relax momentarily, until, involuntarily—I shit. A wet lump begins to bulge in my underwear, unnoticeable to anyone else, thank God. I bolt out of the room and almost miss the arched eyebrows on Mrs. Edmund's face. Students usually must go to the washroom with a buddy, according to Mrs. Edmund.

I hope no one follows me.

"Um, Mrs. Wazalouski, can I go to the washroom?" I beseech in the middle of my grade-four math class as everyone else works. It's the fourth time in school today I've had to ask to use the washroom.

"Abdullah, are you feeling okay?" my teacher asks. "You seem very pale."

"Ah, yes, miss, I just need to…"

My feet scurry out of the room. Stupid bladder. I ain't an old man. I shouldn't be going incontinent for at least another eight decades. All my life I could hold the need to use the washroom for hours on end without a problem.

Now…I don't take the risk. I simply bolt even after a bit of discomfort. It's better to have a slightly unclean toilet than soiled underwear or a ruined reputation—assuming the new vice-principal keeps last week's incident to himself.

Thank goodness the school year is almost over.

Five minutes later, after I finish peeing—four minutes too long—I hobble down the hallway back to class. My legs shake almost violently in my shoes. I lean against the wall—right next to the water fountain. My mouth feels parched. I can only guess it's from all the peeing.

Diagnosed

A part of me says not to drink water right away because it will only cause more trips to the bathroom and disrupt class…the larger part doesn't give a damn.

One hour after I last drank and only minutes after I peed, I spend three more minutes gulping—more like inhaling—a few gallons of water. I feel it swoosh around in my stomach as I stumble back to class—I think I'm gonna regret it.

The car clock reads 3:40 when I heave my bag onto the backseat and sink into the front passenger seat of Mama's bright orange 2003 Nissan Murano.

"*Assalam-u-alaikum* (Peace be upon you), Abdullah!" Mama says, her smile faltering when she looks in my direction. "How was your day?"

"Uh, it was okay, I guess," I reply and look out the window. We managed to get past multiple stop signs on the way during rush hour but we get stuck at Confederation Road, where a sea of cars separates us from our home and my clean washroom. I don't need to go right now. However, if I'm not home in five minutes, then only God knows what might happen.

"You didn't poop your pants again, did you?" Mama asks.

No way to make the question less awkward, I suppose.

"Noooo," I drawl out. "Though I did go to the washroom… like, four times, and drank I don't know how many jugs of water. What's for dinner, Mama? I'm starving…"

"It's not even four yet. I haven't even cooked dinner. Didn't you eat your lunch?"

"I did in the first five minutes….along with the apple and orange you gave me for afternoon snack…"

"And you're hungry again?"

"Yeah…and tired. Class just seem to drag on forever and ever and ever…" A fly buzzes past our car, trudging past the edge of my eyesight, and forward on its journey in the midsummer day heat.

"…talk with your father about this, this doesn't seem to be…"

Oh… right, my mother's saying something… what's Baba got to do with any of this? Why is she talking so fast? Wait… is that our driveway? When did we get past the traffic? Or the other two stop signs? Wasn't it… rush hour just now?

"…Abdullah? Are you even paying attention…" What is Mama yapping on about now?…

The evening of June 12 seems just like any regular night. Summer's arrived and in what's become almost the norm, I slump on my sofa at home. My hands remain limp, my feet dangle off the edge, my face sinks into the soft leathery padding.

"It'll hurt only a…" Mama's voice vaguely echoes through the register of my mind. Baba sits next to her holding a machine, fitted with a small screen and three buttons, with a small strip inserted at the bottom—a glucometer he called it, I think. Baba takes my limp hand in a gentle grip and turns the palm upwards. He wipes a fresh alcohol swab over my right index finger. It glistens in the living room light. Mama blows dry cool air onto the finger.

Baba presses a blue and white device with a hole on one end and a button in the middle against my finger. I feel a prickle of pain, see a small spurt of blood from my fingertip and notice the glucometer sucking in a small fraction of that blood. The machine counts down from five, and then goes ping! I can't see the device from my view, only the slight rising of Baba's face and Mama's deeply furrowed eyebrows.

They test again.

And again.

And again.

They then drag me to Credit Valley Hospital at eleven at night. I just want to sleep, not be kept in a brightly lit room in a thin blue hospital gown amid multiple chattering doctors and nurses…

"…trouble focusing…extreme urination and thirst…extreme fatigue and weakness…extreme hunger…symptoms of diarrhea…"

Somewhere in the haze of urine tests, blood tests, doctor coats and fainting spells from seeing so much blood being sucked out for the first time, I'm told I've been diagnosed with diabetes.

Chapter 5
Diabetes: A Death Sentence

Diabetes: a disease which, in modern times, people joke about catching if they eat too much junk food. Diabetes: the punchline caption hanging below an Instagrammed chocolate cake—diabetes never tasted so good.

Diabetes: a disease which, one hundred years ago, meant a slow, debilitating and inevitable death.

Until Dr. Fredrick Banting discovered insulin in 1921.

What is it?

The Greek physician Aretaeus of Cappadocia first coined the term "diabetes" around nineteen hundred years ago. Diabetes translates to "siphon." As Aretaeus dramatically stated, "No essential part of the drink is absorbed by the body while great masses of the flesh are limbs (liquefied) into urine." The body cannot absorb energy from the food it eats. Instead, it self-cannibalizes its muscles, fats and tissues to obtain tiny morsels of energy.

There remains confusion over who exactly coined the term "mellitus". Some papers credit Dr. Thomas Willis for coining it in 1675. Other papers credit British Surgeon General John Rollo for coining it in 1798.

Regardless, the word *mellitus*—Latin for honey—describes the sweet taste of urine from diabetic individuals. Due to lesser technology and medical expertise, the only way at the time to diagnose someone with diabetes was by taste.

The urine was a defining diagnostic. Under normal circumstances, one does not expect the taste of urine to be anything remotely close to honey. Given that the body didn't absorb any nutrients, it made sense that any sugars consumed would simply waste away in the disposed urine.

Hence physicians used the name *diabetes mellitus*—sweet siphon.

Scientists would not understand or utilize the actual mechanism and physiology behind the disease until over a century later. With medical research and technology quickly advancing, scientists could more closely examine Aretaeus' claim at the microscopic level.

What does diabetes do?

Understanding diabetes mellitus means understanding what it means to not have diabetes. As taught in high-school biology classes, for a nondiabetic, they eat their food and leave absorption and digestion completely to their digestive system.

The stomach mashes the food to a pulp. The small intestine absorbs the fats, carbohydrates, proteins and nutrients. The liver processes everything before ejecting the processed nutrients into the bloodstream.

Now in circulation, cells can take up food and use the different carbohydrates, fats, proteins and nutrients to perform cellular processes.

Among these nutrients, carbohydrates break down into glucose—sugar—molecules. Cells take in glucose and use it alongside oxygen in a process scientists call cellular respiration. Cellular respiration uses glucose and oxygen to make an energy molecule called ATP.

The body uses ATP in an innumerable number of physiological processes. Without ATP, the body will collapse.

Cells must take in glucose for cellular respiration to occur. However, glucose can only enter cells through specific glucose transporters, akin to cell gates. These "gates" need a key to open.

In 1889, Oskar Minkowski and Joseph von Mering, researchers at the University of Strasbourg in France, induced diabetes mellitus in a dog by removing its pancreas. The pancreas must therefore hold the key to treating diabetes. Scientists called this then-hypothesized key insulin. The pancreas produces insulin through a series of island-shaped cells called the islets of Langerhans.

According to the American Diabetes Association, in a diabetic body, the immune system goes rogue, destroying objects it deems foreign and harmful. Through an as-of-yet unknown mechanism, the immune system mistakenly identifies the islets of Langerhans as foreign and harmful. It destroys them in an autoimmune attack.

Without the islets, the pancreas cannot produce insulin. Consequently, all of the glucose that should enter the cells remains trapped in the bloodstream. This causes two main problems:

A surplus and eventually clogging of the bloodstream with glucose molecules, akin to plaque, due to severe hyperglycaemia—high blood glucose levels.

A severe lack of glucose inside the cells.

How does the body react?

To revert hyperglycaemia, the body attempts to autocorrect by filtering the glucose out of the kidneys into urine—known as glycosuria. This causes polyuria—frequent urination.

Frequent urination consequently leads to increased thirst, dehydration and, lastly, damage to the kidneys which are not designed to filter glucose into the urine. During this time, eaten glucose remains inaccessible. Consequently, the body autocorrects via an internal consumption of accessible fats, muscles, proteins and other "nonessential" body resources.

This alternate energy production pathway does yield energy. However, this pathway yields far less energy than the regular glucose-dependant pathway. This energy pathway also makes toxic byproducts called ketones.

Ketones in large enough concentration acidify the blood and bodily fluids. Human beings cannot tolerate acid dropped on our skin. Ketones convert the blood constantly running through our body into acid. This leads to an acute, life-threatening condition known as diabetic ketoacidosis.

Diabetic ketoacidosis, if left untreated, will lead to death.

Undiagnosed diabetics usually display hyperglycaemic symptoms. In the weeks leading up to my own diagnosis, I wet my bed, soiled my pants in class, chugged down gallons of water and suffered from extreme fatigue. This continued for about two weeks until my parents dragged me to the hospital and I fainted.

Was I suffering from diabetic ketoacidosis? If I wasn't already, I probably would have in a few more days. In the current day, diabetic ketoacidosis mandates a trip to the ER. People usually survive.

One hundred years ago, however, diabetic ketoacidosis was always fatal. In fact, it compounded the problem introduced with severe hyperglycaemia. Ketones made the blood acidic. Glucose clogged the blood vessels like plaque and cholesterol. Eating food didn't help the situation. In fact, in most cases, food made it worse.

Diabetes: A Death Sentence

One hundred years ago, patients diagnosed with diabetes didn't suffer only until the diagnosis—no cure or effective treatment existed.

One hundred years ago, diabetes meant a death sentence.

Hospital wards filled with diabetic skeletons draped in skin, completely bedridden. Occasionally, some diabetics regained semiconsciousness before falling back into a coma.

Starving to survive

One hundred years ago, the best treatment for diabetes was a starvation diet published by Dr. Fredrick Allen of the Rockefeller Foundation in New York.

Published in 1919, the diet started with a strict one-week fasting period. During this time, the lack of food would allow the kidneys to slowly filter out surplus glucose through the urine.

Doctors then slowly reintroduced macronutrients like fats, proteins and carbohydrates into the body, and would closely monitor the levels of fat, proteins, carbohydrates and caloric intake.

Doctors would then give food until they detected the glycosuria threshold—when they found glucose in the urine—again. In his findings, Allen gave a diet high on fats and low on carbohydrates.

These diets helped extend diabetic lifespans by a few months.

Source: Gerstein Science Information Centre

Shown above is patient JL, one of the earliest diabetics to receive an insulin injection. The picture on the left shows his state before taking insulin injections. Many diabetics looked like this before the discovery of insulin. The picture on the right depicts him two months later after starting insulin injections.

The good news

Good news, however, came in 1921. By that point, insulin was a hypothesized fluid produced in the pancreas. In 1921, Dr. Fredrick Banting of Canada alongside his colleagues managed to isolate this hypothesized pancreatic extract.

On January 11, 1922, Banting injected insulin into fourteen-year-old Leonard Thompson. By that point, using the Allen diet, a diabetic could exist bedridden or comatose for a few more months, to a couple years at max. Then, they died a painful slow death.

Leonard Thompson died of pneumonia thirteen years later.

Sources:

Allan, F. N. (1972). Diabetes before and after insulin. *Medical History*, *16(3)*, pp. 266–273, http://doi.org/10.1017/S0025727300017750

Diabetes Association, American. (2012). Diagnosis and classification of diabetes mellitus. *Diabetes Care*, *36*(Supplement_1), pp. S67-S74, https://doi.org/10.2337/dc13-s067

Editors, B. (2020). Cellular respiration. *Biology Dictionary*, https://biologydictionary.net/cellular-respiration/

Glycosuria. (2021). *Oxford English Dictionary Online*, https://www.oxfordreference.com/view/10.1093/oi/authority.20110803095856607

Hyperglycaemia. (2021). *Oxford English Dictionary Online*, https://www.oxfordreference.com/view/10.1093/oi/authority.20110803095953902

Karamanou, M., Protogerou A., Tsoucalas G., Androutsos G., & Poulakou-Rebelakou, E. (2016). Milestones in the history of diabetes mellitus: The main contributors. *World Journal Of Diabetes*, *7*(1), https://doi.org/10.4239/wjd.v7.i1.1

Lakhtakia, R. (2013). The history of diabetes mellitus. *Sultan Qaboos University Medical Journal*, *13*(3), pp. 368-370, https://doi.org/10.12816/0003257

Major, R. (2020). The treatment of diabetes mellitus with insulin/The discovery and early development of insulin. Insulin.library.utoronto.ca, https://insulin.library.utoronto.ca/islandora/object/insulin%3AT10183

Polyuria. (2021). *Oxford English Dictionary Online*, https://www.oxfordreference.com/view/10.1093/oi/authority.20110803100336216

Chapter 6
Rice Pudding

I bolt the big brown door shut and enter the walk-in closet. An alcove cabinet embedded into the wall faces me. A decades-old mirror replaces the back wall of the alcove, while a naked light bulb, the only source of light for the entire cubbyhole of a room, protrudes from the right.

A coat rack filled with my family's thick winter coats hides behind the walk-in-closet door. They were made for minus thirty degrees Celsius weather and look out of place in the five degree Celsius Pakistani winter. The walk-in closet connects my parent's room to the washroom.

I open the cabinet and take out a disposable sealed bag with a cartridge and needle, a round blue site insertion set and a vial of insulin. I dump them into the alcove, drop my pants and take out the small blue pager-like insulin pump from my thigh band.

I've been a diabetic for almost two years now. As a diabetic, for whatever stupid reason, my pancreas decided to take a permanent vacation. Without my pancreas, I cannot produce insulin, and without insulin…well, I'd be better off starving to death than eating.

Stupid pancreas.

Because of the deadweight inside me, I have to inject myself with insulin instead. I used to inject myself with needles. A few months ago I switched to an insulin pump.

A pump reduces the amount of injections I need to take. Instead, once every three days, I have to refill my pump with insulin and change the pump's disposable skin patch and tube. I have to keep my pump on 24/7, allowing my body a constant supply of insulin at all times of the day (except when showering).

Keeping a pump on 24/7 probably doesn't feel much different from carrying a phone, I imagine… not that I have a phone. I'm only in grade six. I usually clip the pump to my pant waist or belt and don't keep it incognito inside a thigh band hidden beneath my jeans.

I'm also usually in Canada…*away* from Pakistan. Away from Dada.

I open the pump, take out the empty cartridge and set the pump to rewind. It ran out of insulin a few minutes ago when dinner was about to start.

A whirring sound emanates throughout the room. It's going to take a minute for the pump to rewind. I take out the new cartridge and screw on the disposable needle and blue handle. Flipping the insulin vial upside down, I insert the needle.

With one hand I hold up the vial and with the other I balance the needle and pull down on the handle. The handle doesn't pull down easily. The vial was originally sealed with a certain amount of air and a precise amount of insulin. Take a bit of insulin out and a vacuum forms. I pull down on the handle. A miniature version of tug of war ensues.

"Abdullah!" Phoppoe shouts from the dining room. "Come for dinner!"

My hand slips.

"Coming!" I shout back.

Rice Pudding

I look back at the needle. Damn it. I gave the handle some slack and the vacuum pulled back. The cartridge empties out again into the vial. I pull back once again. The cartridge fills again, slowly.

"Abdullah!" Dadi calls out.

"Dadi, I'm coming!" I shout back.

I hope she heard me. She probably didn't. I don't let go of the handle this time. The cartridge fills fully. I keep it steady with both hands, bite around the vial, and pull.

Ping!

My pump has finished rewinding.

I push the cartridge in and then realize I haven't gotten my new site on. The insertion site remains completely wrapped in its packaging. I quickly examine my old site. It's on my stomach. It seems slightly worn. Part of the adhesive seems to be coming off. I leave the new insertion site sealed.

"Abdullah, you…are a diabetic now." Mama rolled out the phrase slowly after she and Baba sat me down in our living room.

It was the middle of June at the end of grade four. We had just returned from the hospital. I was a freshly diagnosed diabetic. It was a hazy end to the school year. I barely remembered the last few days before my diagnosis. I drank like a fish, peed like a whale and flopped on the couch like a dead man. Oh, and I…had an accident.

"What's a diabetic, Mama?" I had asked.

And why do we need to talk about it right now? I want to sleep!

"It's…it's a condition where the body needs injections to work properly," Baba answered for Mama.

"Wait, wait! I need to poke myself with a NEEDLE every single day!?"

"Once before every meal and twice in the night," Mama replied and showed me the centimetre-long needle. "See, it isn't too big!"

"Um, al-alright, then—"

"Abdullah, you cannot tell your brother that you are diabetic," I recall Baba saying, despite the haze surrounding the memory. I remembered that detail well. Baba looked worried when he said it. Like he knew something I didn't.

"And if he does find out?"

"He might babble about it to someone and they might tell Dada."

A classic case of broken telephone. Brown families and communities have a way of creating very large social circles. Back in Pakistan, practically all of Baba's friends knew Dada and Dadi…and so did their parents and siblings and wives.

Privacy—and for that matter accurate information—does not usually exist in a brown household. While we moved halfway across the world, apparently so did half of Baba's friends. Mention my diabetes to anyone else and twenty chain links later, Dada will be hearing about my funeral last Tuesday.

"But what's so wrong about directly telling Dada? Isn't he a doctor?" I asked Baba.

"He's all the way on the other side of the world, Abdullah. Not only will he worry about you, but he also won't be able to help you here and that will only worry him more."

"But I'll be able to handle myself, won't I? I won't be a cripple or anything because of this, right?"

I don't like being a burden on others. Living with diabetes already seems hard enough! I really hope I don't end up paralyzed or something.

"If only it were that simple," Baba said. He looked over to a picture resting on a nearby table. Dada's portrait stared back. He wasn't smiling.

Rice Pudding

"We need to go shopping for Trendy Kaprey tomorrow, Honneya Baji," Mama tells Phoppoe as I sit down next to my younger cousin Ali. "Apparently, cigarette pants are now in fashion," she scoffs.

Trendy Kaprey is the name of Mama's boutique she runs back at home in Canada, marketing it as *Indo-Pak fashion*—more like "just Pakistani but we need to sound inclusive," she says.

Hopefully no one will ask why I'm late.

Dada sits at the head of the table, his cane resting by his chair, Baba and Phoppa on either side, followed by Mama, Phoppoe, Dadi, Hamza, my cousins Ali and Najla, and me. My last cousin, Ahmed, is absent.

"Rabia, what are cigarette pants?" Dada asks as he devours his rice and chicken.

"It's what everyone else is wearing nowadays, Abu," Mama replies. "Western fashion and all."

Western fashion includes skinny jeans and spaghetti straps, and short shorts and crop tops— everything that goes against Islam's definition of modest clothing.

"Mama, can you pass me a plate?" I ask.

"Sure, what do you want?"

I look around at the dishes. Because we're visiting from Canada for two months, Dadi seems to have gone all out with some of the meals. A bowl filled with *pulao*, brown rice made in chicken broth and served with chicken. A pot at one end of the table swirls with some *nihari*, beef shank meat in stew. The best dish occupies the centre of the table—*paya*, pronounced like "pie," consisting of the gelatinous portions of goat feet in stew.

Naturally, I pick the best dish.

"Paya, please!"

"Finish your food quickly, Abdullah," my grandfather utters through chewed mouthfuls. "Your Dadi made *kheer* (rice pudding) tonight, it's gonna be all gone soon."

"All gone" meaning in his belly.

Everyone chuckles.

It's no secret Dada loves rice pudding.

"Abdullah, what took you so long?" asks Ali slurping on his second cup of Fanta. His plate of rice sits barely touched. His cleats grind out some mud onto the pristine dining hall floor.

Of course, someone noticed I was late.

"Uh, I was in the washroom."

I look away. Mama and Baba sift through their food. Technically, I was in the washroom, only for a second, but I was there. It isn't a lie… barely.

I pick up some naan bread, break a piece, and break some gelatinous meat off the goat foot and place it into the stew. I dip in my naan. Ugh! It's hot. I swish around and find my piece of gelatinous flesh, cup it securely in my naan bread and plop it into my mouth. My hands are sticky from the stew.

"Oh, alright," Ali says. "Here, have some Fanta."

"I'm fine! I usually only drink Diet Coke or Diet Crush, Fanta is too sweet," I say and reach for the water. I sneak a glance at Mama and Baba. They sneak a glance at Dada.

I only drink diet because most regular soda drinks have too much carbohydrates and sugar. I need to keep track of the carbohydrates I eat. Too many carbohydrates and I need that much more insulin, and the more insulin I need, the higher the risk I might overdose, and if I overdose, that will be bad, and it's bad if I underdose. And I'm already gonna have a lot of carbs with tonight's dinner and dessert.

Rice Pudding

"Wait, so you can't have Fanta because it's too sweet?" Dada scrunches his face. "But you used to love Fanta before."

"Uh, yes." I avert my eyes from Dada and force down another bite. My fingers stick together even more. "I just want to be a bit more conscious of the food I eat, that's all!"

"So, you don't want kheer after dinner?"

Oh, no. Oh hell, no. Oh goddamn.

"Hey, where's Ahmed, did he already eat?" I say and ignore Dada's question.

My hands are too sticky. The paya's run out of gelatinous bits. I reach for a tissue.

"He's still exercising outside," Phoppoe responds. "Do you mind telling him to come inside?"

Thank you for the excuse.

"Sure, I'll be back in a bit."

I get up from the table. Baba is already directing Dada to talk about his charity clinic. Ali reaches for his third cup of Coke.

I won't be back in a bit. I'll be back in a while. A long while. I'll get some kheer later when no one is looking.

I return inside after dinner and enter my parents' room. I'm reminded almost immediately of the four cardinal rules my parents told me to always remember.

"Don't check your blood sugar in front of that uncle, he knows Dada and might accidentally tell him." "Don't inject yourself with insulin in front of that auntie, she is a doctor and her parents-in-law know Dada and Dadi." "Don't tell your younger brother, he might blabber it to Dada on Skype." "Whatever you do, DON'T leave your insulin vials out in the open, someone might see them."

Of course, this is the one time I mess up that last cardinal rule, and naturally, that "someone" is Dada.

Shit!

The door to the walk-in-closet is wide open when Dada strolls into my parents' room after dessert, his cane in hand. The entrance to the room is adjacent to the walk-in-closet.

All Dada needs to do is turn ninety degrees to his left and find the insulin vials and unopened insertion set I left out in the open when rushing to dinner nested in the walk-in-closet shelf.

I hate keeping secrets, especially from my family. We're probably not the only family in the world keeping a disease like diabetes a secret. But it's been two years and I still don't understand why. Why would it be so bad if Dada found out?

More pressingly however, how do I get past Dada and hide the insulin vials? Whatever the reason, all I know is if Dada finds out right now, this family vacation will most probably be ruined.

"Abu, you haven't tried this *luddu* (a sweet)," Baba almost shouts from behind me. His voice is really close to panicking. "It's really good!"

Dada's face lights up as he registers my dad's claim.

"Impossible! The best luddus are stored in my room." It appears Dada's sweet tooth will never unsweeten. "Come, those sweets aren't going to finish themselves! But bring those you have with you as well. I need to see how good your luddus are."

He turns around and hurries towards his room. In his haste, his eyes skip over the vials still in the closet. I dash to the walk-in closet, grab the vials and stash them inside my pant pocket. I run into Mama on my way out. I gulp.

Stupid Abdullah!

I don't think I'm having any rice pudding tonight. I don't deserve it.

Chapter 7

Highs and Lows

Diabetes: A disease where a person used to be starved of all sugars and sweets, rice and wheats. Where starvation was used not to execute death but to prolong life. Where starvation was the only way to turn limp, bedridden hours and days into maybe a couple of numbing months or years.

If vampires were real, they would have diabetics for dessert. Diabetic blood would be overloaded with sugar incapable of entering tissues, sugar that formed blockages in the bloodstream, sugar that hindered oxygen transport, leading to cell death.

Death approached whether one tried or didn't try to stave it off; either too much sugar suffocated your system to death, or too little sugar starved your organs to collapse.

Diabetes: A disease for which multiple summer camps are set up all around Canada. Camps where children spend a week or two or four away from home, away from parents (yay!), with other diabetics, and goof off in the summer sun.

Diabetes: A disease so unknown before the twentieth century, yet so ancient, that the only way to ascertain whether one had it in Ancient Rome was by tasting one's urine and describing the pale-yellow froth of waste as sweet as honey. A disease for which there is no known cure, only a treatment of synthetically grown insulin to replace what the pancreas cannot produce.

Camp: A place for children who, just as it was a hundred years ago, feel sick when high on sugar, but who now, also feel sick when they give themselves too much insulin when they go low on sugar.

At camp, I tend to go low and keep going low. I can handle it now after eleven years' worth of experience. The weakness as I walk. The sluggishness as I move. The feeling one gets when they wake up in bed, sometimes at three in the morning, in sweat-soaked shirts.

The problem with experience: one isn't bothered as much by the symptoms—or as aware of them. Doctors call this hypoglycaemic unawareness—where the body goes low on sugar, but cannot sense it.

The Frisbee whizzes past Hayden. I catch it. Going low, I sprint past Vic, and then fire it off to Jamie.

My heart beats fast. Thump. Thump. Thump.

I steady my legs. I'm a little more tired than I thought. I shouldn't be surprised. I've always had weak stamina. I'll just rest for a bit.

"Hey, folks! Y'all continue on. I'm gonna take a small breather!" I yell as I walk towards the shade under a single thick tree in the humid August afternoon. My breath deepens. Yeah, just slightly tired.

I notice a low-kit with a glucometer and dextrose sugar tablets laying on the ground a metre away. I ran around quite a lot in ten minutes. It wouldn't hurt to see if I'm going low.

Highs and Lows

If anything, I can get some delicious orange dextrose tablets. Going low means going under 4.0 millimolars of sugar. If you get to 3.0, that's urgent. Often at camp, because of the increased activity, I would usually somehow end up at 2.4.

I estimated my blood sugar to be around 3.9 millimolar.

I check in at 1.8.

I somehow remain fully conscious as my friend Jen walks me to the med cabin to see the doctors. Were I not conscious, I would have been glucked—given a dose of glucagon to flare up my blood sugar. Usually, the body of a nondiabetic would do this automatically—send glucagon from the pancreas to the liver, demand the release of stored sugar, and done! For diabetics, glucagon is injected in only the most severe of circumstances—a last resort—before the hospital.

Camp: A place where if you do end up having a seizure—when you're as close to 0.0 as possible and your brain starts to quit—there won't be a pair of parents worried to death.

There won't be a pair of parents who, when they hear your arms and legs banging on the bathroom floor, will teleport to your room to find a headless chicken jolting around, head and brain still asleep, like the dead man he would have become had he been alone.

You won't feel like you woke up in a dream and when you realize it isn't a dream, you won't be confused about why you fell asleep Friday night at your house and woke up Saturday morning in a hospital bed.

No. At camp, you'll have a plethora of doctors and an armada of nurses all trained to take professional care of you. No one will worry in an uncontrolled panic, but rather to go through the necessary steps to ensure your wellbeing and to calmly explain to you when you wake up what you went through.

Camp: A place where you don't have to go to the bathroom away from everyone else to check your blood sugar and inject yourself.

Where you aren't asked why you prick your finger for blood or how you manage to inject yourself multiple times a day.

Where you don't have to explain whether you can eat a doughnut or not (you can!) or why you are eating a sugary snack when you go low. Rather, camp is a place where everyone pricks their fingers for blood together.

Where everyone gleefully eyes the new flavours of dex tabs and hope to go ever so slightly low enough to try them.

Where campers inject insulin together and don't have to explain to anyone that they do it because they want to live.

Where first-time self-injectors are given shout-outs after evening snack, followed by a volley of cheers in the lines of R-O-C-K-YOU-ROCK-YOU-ROCK! or S-U-P-E-R-SUPER-SUPER-THAT'S-WHAT-YOU-ARE! or WE-ARE-PROUD-OF-YOU!

The cheers aren't simply to cheer a person up. They are the truth. Yes, my friend, you do rock! You are super!! And everyone is mighty damn proud of you!!!

Chapter 8

The Bloody Problem With Glucose Testing

In 2012, Dr. Maria Teodorczyk at California's Lifescan Inc.'s research and development department introduced the OneTouch Verio, a new blood glucose meter (glucometer). This device ameliorates problems previous glucose monitors encountered when used by the elderly, as well as for premature babies, in treating their *diabetes mellitus*.

What is diabetes mellitus?

Diabetes mellitus involves the regulation and intake of the carbohydrates we consume from our meals. Biologists know this regulation as *glucose homeostasis*.

Carbohydrates break down into their subunits, glucose, after digestion. Glucose constantly flows through the blood stream. The body needs glucose to create usable energy molecules called ATP. When needed, the pancreas secretes the hormone insulin.

Insulin acts like a key, opening cell gates to allow glucose entry into individual cells.

Diabetes mellitus occurs when the body runs into problems concerning glucose homeostasis and insulin regulation. The American Diabetes Association divides diabetes mellitus into two major subtypes: type 1 and type 2.

Type 1 occurs when the key is lost: the pancreas can no longer produce insulin. Type 2 occurs when the cell gates rust away: the body develops insulin resistance. The pancreas can no longer regulate glucose homeostasis in either case. Manual diagnosis becomes mandatory.

Manual diagnosis: glucometers

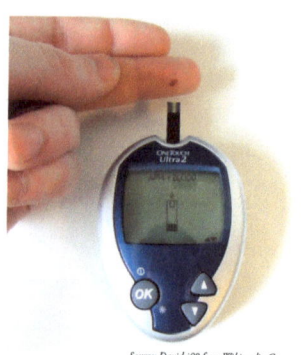

Source: David-i98 from Wikimedia Commons
A diabetic inserts a drop of blood into the test strip capillary of a glucometer for a blood glucose test.

Diabetics today rely heavily on glucometers to accurately detect states of glucose or glycemic emergencies.

Glucometers pair with disposable, insertable test strips. These test strips possess a small capillary of a cavity. This capillary acts as a surface for multiple chemicals and enzymes to remain suspended.

Enzymes (biological proteins) serve as catalysts. These catalysts help to nudge and accelerate molecules down specific chemical pathways.

The capillary sucks in a small blood sample drawn from a fingertip. A lancet—a small poking device—pricks the skin, letting a droplet of blood escape from the fingertip capillaries.

When sucked into the capillary, an enzyme called glucose oxidase transforms the glucose in the blood into a substance called gluconic acid. The gluconic acid then combines with a compound called ferricyanide to form ferrocyanide, an electrically conductive compound.

Running electricity from the glucometer through the test strip forms a current that travels through the available ferrocyanide. Larger amounts of ferrocyanide induce a stronger current. Larger amounts of ferrocyanide corresponds to a larger quantity of glucose available in the blood sample.

Hence, a stronger current translates to a higher blood glucose concentration and a lower current translates to a lower blood glucose concentration. Diabetics can thus adjust their insulin dose and meal intake accordingly.

However, through this test, problems can cause incorrect glucose measurements. Incorrect measurements cause a diabetic to make choices which unknowingly throw glucose homeostasis into disarray. Failure to maintain glucose homeostasis results in one of two possible conditions: *hyperglycaemia* or *hypoglycaemia*.

Glucose control out of whack: why so serious?

Scientists define hyperglycaemia as a state of surplus glucose circulating the blood stream. This surplus, if not cut down to normal levels, can induce longterm, chronic complications like blindness and nerve damage, as a result of the glucose acting like aggressive plaque. Extreme complications can lead to fatality.

Scientists define hypoglycaemia as a state of insufficient glucose circulating the blood stream. This deficiency, if not raised to normal levels, can cause shortterm, acute emergencies like seizures and comas. Untreated emergencies can lead to fatality.

In the past few years, a component of blood called the hematocrit attributed to many incorrect glucometer measurements.

Hematocrit: the literal blood cell count

Hematocrit is the portion of whole blood composed solely of *erythrocytes* (red blood cells). While usually there is no distinction between red blood cells (RBCs) and the rest of the blood plasma, a centrifuge can separate whole blood into its individual components for scientific analysis.

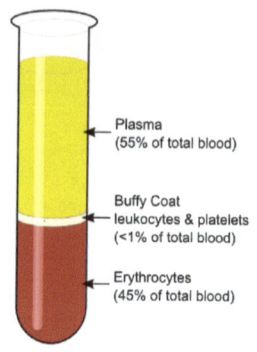

Source: KnuteKnudsen from Wikimedia Commons
Centrifuged whole blood separates into its separate components. Of these, erythrocytes make up about 45% of the entire blood volume. This is the hematocrit.

A centrifuge spins a blood sample at high velocities, allowing the individual components to separate based on how heavy they are. Healthy individuals often have hematocrit making up 36%-53% of their total blood volume.

However, hematocrit actually interferes with blood glucose testing. The RBCs serve as a physical blockade. They can be likened to a rowdy crowd, through which a glucose molecule must cross in order to reach a glucose oxidase enzyme.

Hence, only some glucose molecules manage to reach the glucose oxidase enzyme instead of all of them. Higher hematocrit concentrations would thus lead to falsely lowered glucose readings.

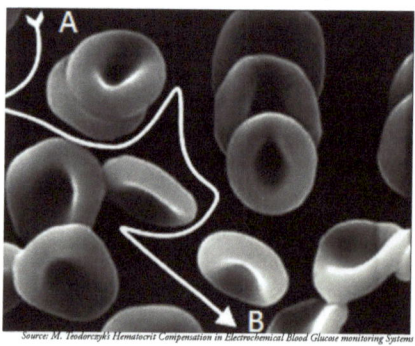

Source: M. Teodorczyk's Hematocrit Compensation in Electrochemical Blood Glucose monitoring Systems
The RBCs of the hematocrit act like a rowdy crowd, making it difficult for glucose molecules to reach the glucose oxidase enzyme.

Glucometers do account for a standardized hematocrit concentration. Such a concentration exists in healthy adults.

However, research by scientists Martha and Andrew Lyon in Alberta, Canada, shows that this number varies drastically in certain scenarios.

It varies immensely if a person is sick and elderly, and being very low relative to the average. It varies immensely with a neonate, a premature baby, being very high relative to the average.

With a high hematocrit count, many glucose molecules cannot react with glucose oxidase. Hence, neonates with diabetes would have falsely lowered blood glucose readings. This would lead to doctors giving the neonate less insulin than needed and lead to chronic hyperglycaemia and possibly even longterm complications.

The diabetic elderly, on the other hand, would have falsely elevated glucose readings, because not enough hematocrit would impede glucose molecules as expected by the preprogrammed test strip. This would lead to the elderly taking more insulin than required and lead to a hypoglycaemic emergency and possible fatality.

Dr. Teodorczyk and her team thus devised a unique test strip and computer algorithm. They focused their efforts on graphing the physical distance and time it took for the different components of the test reaction to reach completion.

Different amounts of hematocrit would cause variations in these times and graphs. Dr. Teodorczyk then used these values to adjust *any* raw blood glucose readings that effectively accounts for the unique hematocrit composition from person to person.

Sources:

Centrifugation. (2021). *Oxford English Dictionary Online*, https://www.oxfordreference.com/view/10.1093/oi/authority.20110803095558781

Clarke, S., & Foster, J. (2012). A history of blood glucose meters and their role in self-monitoring of diabetes mellitus. *British Journal Of Biomedical Science*, *69*(2), pp. 83-93, https://doi.org/10.1080/09674845.2012.12002443

David-i98 (Photographer). *The process of blood glucose testing* [digital image], https://commons.wikimedia.org/wiki/File:Blood_Glucose_Testing.JPG

Diabetes Association, American. (2012). Diagnosis and classification of diabetes mellitus. *Diabetes Care*, *36*(Supplement_1), pp. S67-S74, https://doi.org/10.2337/dc13-s067

Editors, B. (2020). Cellular respiration. *Biology Dictionary*, https://biologydictionary.net/cellular-respiration/

Haematocrit. (2021). *Oxford English Dictionary Online*, https://www.oxfordreference.com/view/10.1093/oi/authority.20110803095914990

Hönes, J., Müller, P., & Surridge, N. (2008). The technology behind glucose meters: Test strips. *Diabetes Technology & Therapeutics*, *10*(s1), pp. S-10-S-26, https://doi.org/10.1089/dia.2008.0005

Hyperglycaemia. (2021). *Oxford English Dictionary Online*, https://www.oxfordreference.com/view/10.1093/oi/authority.20110803095953902

Hypoglycaemia. (2021). *Oxford English Dictionary Online*, https://www.oxfordreference.com/view/10.1093/oi/authority.20110803095954516

Knudsen, Knute. (Photographer). Scheme of a blood sample after centrifugation [digital image], https://en.wikipedia.org/wiki/File:Blood-centrifugation-scheme.png

Lyon, M., & Lyon, A. (2011). Patient acuity exacerbates discrepancy between whole blood and plasma methods through error in molality to molarity conversion: "Mind the gap!" *Clinical Biochemistry*, *44*(5-6), pp. 412-417, https://doi.org/10.1016/j.clinbiochem.2011.01.005

Rao, L., Jakubiak, F., Sidwell, J., Winkelman, J., & Snyder, M. (2005). Accuracy evaluation of a new glucometer with automated hematocrit measurement and correction. *Clinica Chimica Acta*, *356*(1-2), pp. 178-183, https://doi.org/10.1016/j.cccn.2005.01.027

Teodorczyk, M., Cardosi, M., & Setford, S. (2012). Hematocrit compensation in electrochemical blood glucose monitoring systems. *Journal Of Diabetes Science And Technology*, *6*(3), pp. 648-655, https://doi.org/10.1177/193229681200600320

Tirimacco, R., Siew, L., Simpson, P., Cowley, P., & Tideman, P. (2014). Understanding the Hematocrit effect on glucose testing using popular point-of-care testing devices. *Point Of Care: The Journal Of Near-Patient Testing & Technology*, *13*(4), pp. 128-131, https://doi.org/10.1097/poc.0000000000000040

Tonyushkina, K., & Nichols, J. (2009). Glucose meters: A review of technical challenges to obtaining accurate results. *Journal Of Diabetes Science And Technology*, *3*(4), pp. 971-980, https://doi.org/10.1177/193229680900300446

Chapter 9
CGMS: Video Recorders Not Snapshot Cameras

In 2000, Doctors Kerstin Rebrin and Garry Steil conducted a study investigating the dynamic relationship between blood and the interstitial fluid surrounding it. They wanted to see if interstitial fluid could replace whole blood as a medium for monitoring the glucose levels of a person suffering from diabetes mellitus.

What is diabetes mellitus?

Diabetes mellitus remains one of the most prominent diseases of the twenty-first century. According to the American Diabetes Association, diabetes mellitus occurs when the body can no longer uphold one of its main regulatory functions: glucose homeostasis.

Glucose homeostasis refers to the uptake and regulation of the carbohydrates we eat. Carbohydrates break down into a sugar called glucose and continuously circulate the bloodstream. The body cells consume glucose to generate usable energy called ATP.

However, body cells cannot simply swallow glucose as we swallow a sandwich. Body cell walls act like locked gates. These locked gates require a specific key to allow glucose entry: the hormone insulin. Insulin production occurs in the pancreas.

Glucose homeostasis maintains a fine balance between the amount of sugar in the bloodstream and the amount of sugar in the cells. Glucose homeostasis works according to a "Goldilocks principle."

Hyperglycaemia describes a body overflowing with blood-circulating glucose. *Hypoglycaemia* describes a glucose-starved body. Both throw glucose homeostasis into disarray for different reasons.

Hyperglycaemia clogs the bloodstream with glucose, akin to aggressive plaque. Clogged blood vessels, if not cleared, lead to chronic complications like blindness and nerve damage. Extreme complications can lead to fatality.

Hypoglycaemia clears the bloodstream of glucose, often due to too much insulin or too much energy expenditure. Cleared blood vessels, if not given glucose, can lead to acute emergencies like seizures and comas. Untreated emergencies can lead to fatality.

Hence, glucose homeostasis maintains a "Goldilocks zone" in between these two extremes.

A healthy pancreas in a healthy body can successfully manage glucose homeostasis. The pancreas easily detects hyperglycaemic and hypoglycaemic events and corrects them back to normal levels. A nondiabetic does not need to calculate how much carbohydrates they will consume in a meal. A nondiabetic does not need to signal to their pancreas to input a proportionate amount of insulin.

An unhealthy pancreas in a diabetic body cannot successfully manage glucose homeostasis. Glucose homeostasis, then, falls on manual diagnosis and treatment.

CGMS: Video Recorders Not Snapshot Cameras

Blood glucose monitors and their limitations

The caveat with diagnosing different blood glucose concentrations lies in the current limitations many technologies possess. Obtaining truly accurate blood glucose readings can only happen at hospitals and laboratories, where scientists can separate and analyze blood in detail.

Diabetics do not have complete laboratories set up at home. Instead, since the tail end of the twentieth century, portable glucose monitors or glucometers allow reasonably accurate glucose estimations at home.

Glucometers work via an electrochemical process that transforms a chemical or biological signal into an electrical signal. For glucometers, their electrochemical processes happen on a test strip. The test strip contains a small blood-sucking capillary suspended with multiple chemicals and biological proteins called enzymes. Enzymes function as catalysts, molecules which help facilitate a chemical reaction, but remain separate from the final product.

For a glucometer to function, a person pokes their finger with a lancet, a small finger-poking device. The capillary sucks in a small fraction of poked blood. In the capillary, the enzyme glucose oxidase transforms glucose found in blood into a substance called gluconic acid. Gluconic acid then combines with a suspended chemical called ferricyanide to form ferrocyanide, an electrically conductive compound.

The glucometer then conducts a current through the ferrocyanide. While a fixed current enters the test strip, a variable current exits depending on the amount of available ferrocyanide. The more ferrocyanide available, the larger the current.

As more glucose creates more ferrocyanide, a larger current translates to a larger blood glucose concentration. However, while effective and accurate, glucometers remain limited in two major ways.

First, diabetics must check their blood glucose multiple times per day. Each time, diabetics must pierce their finger and draw out a small droplet of blood. They must check before each meal. They must check when they feel blood glucose levels dipping too low or soaring too high. Even without symptoms, good practice remains to check blood glucose levels every two to four hours.

Blood glucose levels may also necessitate a check or two in the night to make sure no emergencies slip by undetected. Parental fear for their child's safety may very well magnify this problem whereby parents check too often during the night. This disrupts the sleep of all parties involved.

As a diabetic, I can attest that such a routine can take a mental toll on both the diabetic and their family members.

Second, while glucometers continue to rise in accuracy with technological advancements, they can give only a snapshot of the present moment. Glucometers work like cameras. They provide good photos (results). However, in between photos, diabetics may miss crucial events and dynamic glucose trends.

In such a situation, Thomas Gray's famous phrase "Ignorance is bliss" does not apply. For diabetics, ignorance does not induce bliss. Ignorance induces fear. In such a situation, perpetual knowledge of a diabetic's blood glucose levels would induce bliss. As such, compared to a snapshot camera like a glucometer, a video recorder may present a more complete picture. In this case, a video recorder would continuously capture blood glucose levels 24/7.

Yet no one would want blood constantly drawn from them every five minutes. How could such a video recorder manifest into reality? In the past two decades, companies like Medtronic, Dexcom and Abbott monopolized on the idea of a constant glucose reader.

CGMS: Video Recorders Not Snapshot Cameras

Since 1999, these companies focused either part or all of their research on making such "video recorders," or Continuous Glucose Monitoring Systems (CGMS) a reality.

CGMSs assemble as a transmitter on a disposable patch inserted onto the skin. A one-time-use insertion set helps pierce the skin, leaving a minuscule tube called a cannula right below the skin. The cannula functions akin to a test strip, filled with enzymes like glucose oxidase, measuring glucose levels in the surrounding area.

Unlike a blood glucometer, however, the cannula does not penetrate blood vessels and measure blood directly. Instead, the cannula penetrates the interstitial fluid, which surrounds cells and act like a support structure. Water and various compounds comprise the interstitial fluid. It allows certain compounds and minerals to diffuse out of the bloodstream. One of these compounds the circulating blood is glucose.

A CGMS measures this interstitial fluid glucose level. Because the cannula stays inserted continuously, the CGMS transmits these glucose readings throughout the day. However, given that interstitial fluid glucose levels are not blood glucose levels, there must be a difference between the readings, right?

The difference explored:

In 2000, Doctors Kerstin Rebrin and Garry Steil explored this difference. They used data obtained from the Medtronic MiniMed CGMS, the first CGM produced in 1999.

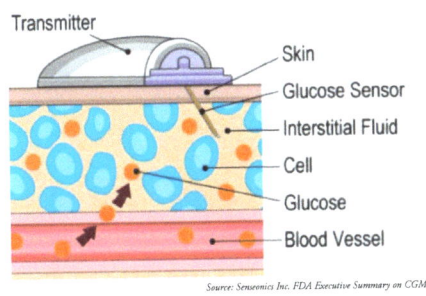

Source: Sensionics Inc. FDA Executive Summary on CGMS

A CGM remains inserted on a patch. The glucose sensor, contained in a hollow tube called a cannula, gives interstitial fluid glucose measurements instead of blood glucose measurements. Dr. Rebrin and Dr. Steil focused experiments on determining if this approach was feasible.

Utilizing this data, they concluded that there exists a delay of about five to twelve minutes between blood glucose measurements and interstitial fluid glucose measurements. This delay occurs because the glucose molecules take time to diffuse out of the blood stream and into the interstitial fluid.

Drs. Rebrin and Steil also conducted a simulation study based on this data. A simulation study is a computer experiment. It uses data and a computer algorithm to arrive at a theoretical estimation. Through this simulation study, they modelled a situation where interstitial fluid replaced whole blood as a medium for holding glucose molecules. Through this simulation, they estimated that the interstitial fluid glucose value would be extremely erroneous six percent of the time.

Utilizing this data, they concluded that the structural and functional properties of interstitial fluid would not pose a significant obstacle in using it as an alternative to blood glucose measurements.

The present:

Source: Mike Huskins on Healthline

A CGMS graph gives glucose measurements every five minutes, 24/7. The grey area depicts the "Goldilocks Zone." Diabetics want to maintain their blood sugar levels within this Goldilocks Zone.

CGMSs in the early twenty-first century, while novel, could only serve as an adjunctive therapy, an add-on to glucometer testing and finger-pricking instead of outright replacing it. This largely resulted from the less refined technology used. CGMSs could not give as accurate of a reading as glucometers. They could indicate general trends and help lower the number of glycemic emergencies. Fortunately, in 2015, the US FDA approved CGMSs from companies like Dexcom as replacements to glucometers due to a sufficiently increased accuracy.

Sources:

Diabetes Association, American. (2012). Diagnosis and classification of diabetes mellitus. *Diabetes Care*, *36*(Supplement_1), pp. S67-S74, https://doi.org/10.2337/dc13-s067

Editors, B. (2020). Cellular respiration. *Biology Dictionary*, https://biologydictionary.net/cellular-respiration/

Gray, T. (2020). Ode on a Distant Prospect of Eton College. *Poetry Foundation*, https://www.poetryfoundation.org/poems/44301/ode-on-a-distant-prospect-of-eton-college.

Hönes, J., Müller, P., & Surridge, N. (2008). The technology behind glucose meters: Test strips. *Diabetes Technology & Therapeutics*, *10*(s1), pp. S-10-S-26, https://doi.org/10.1089/dia.2008.0005

Hoskins, M. (2020). *News: FDA approves the Dexcom G6 CGM!* Healthline, https://www.healthline.com/diabetesmine/newsflash-fda-oks-dexcom-g6-cgm.

Hyperglycaemia. (2021). *Oxford English Dictionary Online*, https://www.oxfordreference.com/view/10.1093/oi/authority.20110803095953902

Hypoglycaemia. (2021). *Oxford English Dictionary Online*, https://www.oxfordreference.com/view/10.1093/oi/authority.20110803095954516

Rebrin, K., & Steil, G. (2000). Can interstitial glucose assessment replace blood glucose measurements? *Diabetes Technology & Therapeutics*, *2*(3), pp. 461-472, https://doi.org/10.1089/15209150050194332

Tonyushkina, K., & Nichols, J. (2009). Glucose meters: A review of technical challenges to obtaining accurate results. *Journal Of Diabetes Science And Technology*, *3*(4), pp. 971-980, https://doi.org/10.1177/193229680900300446

Senseonics, Inc. (2018). FDA executive summary, https://www.fda.gov/media/112110/download

Chapter 10

Aging Ears and Aging Years

"Abdullah!" Baba calls from the TV room. "Come down! It's Dada!"

"Coming!" I jolt up from my study table. It's strange. On most days, Baba would probably text or call me on my phone. He would only directly shout for me if it's something urgent. I hope everything's alright.

"*Assalam-u-alikum* (Peace be Upon you), Dada!" I greet my grandfather over the phone. It isn't quite a yell. I try to be as loud as politely possible. I don't know how well he can hear me.

"*Walaikum-salam* (Peace be upon you as well), Abdullah." He pauses. "How are you?"

"I'm fine! Just got a test for grade-nine science I was studying for."

Whenever I tell Mama "I have a quiz next week" it somehow becomes "he has a test in a few days" when she tells Baba.

By some literal version of broken telephone, "test" morphs into "Abdullah's been busy studying day in day out for a final exam he's taking in two days. Please pray for him!" by the time Baba tells our family back home. I'm surprised I haven't so far been told "good luck!" for an upcoming United States Medical Licensing Examination I'm supposedly about to take in an hour.

"How are you, Dada?"

"Abdullah, your dadi recently told me you are diabetic."

Wait. Hold up. My head jerks over to Baba. He nods. He remains still. I don't think he expected this call today either.

"Yes, Dada, I-I am diabetic, I've, uh, been so for almost"—I count the years on my fingers—"five years now."

Dada's voice is slow. Quiet. Delayed.

"Are...are you managing it alright?"

"Yes. I've kept it in check. It sometimes spikes or dips a bit, but I handle it quickly enough. Mama and Baba help a lot, too. There's nothing to worry about at all."

My grin strains. It isn't a lie, technically speaking.

"Alright, that's good to hear. If you need any help, just call me. I'll be a phone and a plane ticket away."

"I will. Thank you."

"Can you pass the phone to your baba? I need to talk to him."

"Sure. Baba, Dada wants to talk to you."

My father takes the phone. I speed walk to the stairs. That seems to have gone well. Dada took it better than you thought, Baba, I think to myself.

"Haroon, it's been *five* years?" Dada's voice booms over the phone speaker.

I make a detour from the stairs and head towards the kitchen. A glass of water sounds nice right about now. A glass of water from the kitchen, next to the TV lounge where Baba sits. I drag my feet into the kitchen.

"Abu, we didn't want you to worry—"

"I AM A DOCTOR! Don't you think I can handle something like this?"

Aging Ears and Aging Years

"Abu, he was a fourth grader who freaked out over needles when we told him." Baba grinds his molars as he tries to keep his voice steady. In Islam, parents must be given respect in practically all scenarios, even when they are yelling. Naturally, this isn't always easy

"If you would have told me about him—."

"If we told you about him what would you have done?" Baba jumps in. "Rabia and I, we already worried about him every night and every day, and that's when we were with him. You know more than anyone else what a diabetic goes through, Abu. You're diabetic yourself!" Baba's voice rises slightly. He takes a second to calm himself down. "Sure he's type one and you're type two, but you know what they go through. More importantly, you would have focused on what diabetics used to go through. And what they still go through in Pakistan."

Dada was a doctor in the twentieth century. The only experiences with type one diabetics he remembers probably clash with how he has seen me act, eating sweets and staying up late. Beyond that, to have diabetes or "sugar" in Pakistan as everyone calls it there, would stigmatize a young diabetic as a "cripple." Perhaps a hundred years ago a diabetic was a "cripple."

That isn't the case today. Not by a longshot.

"You don't know that," Dada mutters. "Whatever—just keep me up to date on anything that comes up with him. Got it?"

"Yes, Abu."

I take a small plastic cup from the cupboard and fill it with water. I gulp it down. I toss the cup into the sink and head up the stairs. I reach my room and sprawl on my bed. Allen's juice boxes, for emergency use only, lie beside it.

I hate Allen's.

Four empty juice boxes lie scattered on the table next to it, plastic straws and wrappers strewn about, the only evidence of last night's hypoglycemic attack. I gave myself too much insulin.

I miscalculated—badly. My blood sugar level dropped. Not dipped. Dropped. The stupid juice brand has a horrible taste—and worse aftertaste—but for some reason it's the only juice Mama can find every single time she buys juice boxes.

Last night she practically shoved the juice down my throat before I woke up and drank it on my own. She panics easily. I don't blame her. I woke up and treated my hypo.

Hypoglycemic sugar levels cause weakness. If severe enough, hypoglycemic sugar levels can cause seizures. Which can lead to comas. Which if left undetected and untreated can cause death.

Last April I went to bed at home on Friday night and woke up Saturday morning in Credit Valley Hospital with no idea how I got there. They tell me I was sent there after supposedly flopping around like a headless chicken and banging the bathroom wall in the early morning.

I don't think I'll ever tell Dada about that one.

Never.

Some things are better left unsaid.

Chapter 11

Walker

Surgery

Dada visits Canada in May 2015 to meet his favourite grandchildren, Hamza and I, and to catch-up with his only son and daughter-in-law who live halfway across the world.

He also visits to have open heart surgery to bypass a blocked artery.

Senility

Dada's room on the first floor is the entire reason why we moved houses in the first place. There was no other reason to move three hundred metres away into a slightly bigger, slightly more expensive house. Dada's room, a small den with double doors directly opposite the living room, allows space for a queen-size bed, a nightstand and my old study table and leather office chair.

He spends the days before his surgery reacquainting himself with Canada. In the morning Dada gets up early, says the Fajr morning prayer before dawn, and spends the next few hours at his table reading and highlighting his Quran in blue, yellow and red. At eighty years old, senility still hasn't reached him.

Paranoia

"He constantly asks me how Ali's studies are coming, or if Ahmed's still strumming his days away on his guitar, or what I did today, or what Naveed's been doing, or if the servants are behaving," I hear Honneya phoppoe say to Baba one night. "He's getting more paranoid, Haroon. It isn't a good thing."

"It's..." Baba pauses. "It's a similar situation here. He constantly asks about Abdullah's blood sugar levels, if he's okay and when he last ate." Baba sighs. I understand now. Dada loves to be in the loop, to be in control. Had we told him about my diagnosis when I could barely comprehend it myself, Dada's world would've crumbled long ago. There never was a good time to spill the secret. Not to Dada.

"Can you try to calm him down somewhat?" Phoppoe's voice betrays her exhaustion. "Every time I talk to him, it's more like an interrogation than an actual conversation."

"Don't worry, he'll be busy with his heart surgery soon enough. His interrogations will be the least of our concerns." Baba takes a deep breath. "Please pray his surgery goes without any complications." His voice shakes.

"*Inshallah* (God willing), he will be fine, have faith."

"Inshallah."

Like Mona Lisa

One evening, we visit Abrar uncle's house in Pickering. Abrar uncle is one of those family friends my parents have known since forever. We're part of a circle of families who, besides us, all have some direct link to each other, whether by sisters or brothers or grandfathers and grandmothers.

By this time a black beard and a thin moustache, both overgrown and unkempt, cover my face. My moustache trails over my lip. Mama is mad.

"Abdullah, you must trim your beard! You must look presentable. Yet here you are looking like you just walked out of the jungle!"

I think my beard, which curls against my chin, is too short. It isn't even a full beard yet, and not nearly as dense as Dada's beard—packed, straight, completely white and matches his still-perfect silky hair.

Ugh! Why does my beard curl up before growing out!?

I rush to the washroom and trim my beard from the top down. I don't do it often but I think I do a pretty decent job. Not a lot of hair falls off. I look into the mirror and brush my hand through my beard to get rid of any stray strands of cut hair.

"Abdullah, you haven't trimmed your beard yet?" Mama says when I reach downstairs again.

"I just did!"

"Haroon!" Mama motions to Baba. "Look, does that look even close to set? He hasn't even gotten the line right!"

Baba turns my head left, then right and looks underneath my chin. "You're right. Abdullah, bring your trimmer downstairs, I'll—"

"Let me do it this time," Dada says. "I have much more experience and can sculpt your beard to perfection!"

I suppress a groan and drag myself up the stairs again to retrieve my trimmer. There is no arguing with Baba. There is definitely no arguing with Dada.

A few moments later, I sit on a stool in front of Dada in the TV lounge. I'm slightly taller than Dada, who sinks into his seat, making him eye-level with my beard. Perfect. I place my hands by my sides, hold the leather cushion and wrap my long legs around the stool's legs.

Dada takes note of my beard from all sides. He turns on the trimmer. A vibrational hum fills the silence. A towel lies in his lap, positioned beneath my face, a barrier between my falling hair and the carpet below.

Dada's tongue sticks out slightly and his eyes narrow. His hand slowly brings the trimmer to my neck, then gently pulls from the bottom up. A swath of hair falls onto the towel. Then another. And another. Dada removes the number two clip from the trimmer and then begins trimming again. I hope he's just making a beard line.

My nose itches. My head itches. I keep still. I don't want even a single distraction to potentially ruin my beard. I feel like the Mona Lisa must have felt when she was being painted—agonizingly still, probably with an urge to itch some hair and with no idea how it would turn out.

When I look at myself in the mirror, I realize Dada is no Da Vinci.

Although I try not to show it, my parents don't think much of my frown. It's like the reverse of Mona Lisa's smile—barely visible, unless you look closely.

At Abrar uncle's house, as always, there is some function relating to one of his five daughters and a soon-to-be wedding. A function where pictures are taken and taken and then taken again three more times. When the pictures are shown later that day, however, I compare my new look with my old.

Dada is no Da Vinci. But he's good enough.

Four weeks

Dada's surgery takes seven hours—three hours longer than it should. Mama and Baba spend the day at the hospital. At night, Mama returns home and says the doctors think Dada should be out in a week. She looks after Dada during the day. Baba stays with him every single night.

Walker

Dada is discharged from the hospital four weeks after he was admitted. Baba returns home with a permanently ruined sleep cycle.

Walker

When Dada returns home he finds his cane can no longer support him. He needs a walker. He has hated his walker ever since a nurse started him on his physical rehabilitation and had to walk with him.

"I don't need your help! I don't want this walker! I just need my cane!" he once said to his nurse when I visited the hospital with Mama after school. The nurse ignored him and smiled.

Dada still goes to the washroom on his own. He still comes to dinner on his own.

One day while I'm up late working on a school assignment in my room upstairs, I hear a thud from below.

I rush down. Mama and Baba rush over from their sofa-bed in the TV lounge. Hamza stays fast asleep.

Dada lies on the ground, his feet extended, his back still slightly propped up against his bed.

Sleep intermingles with hot tears, burning through his eyes.

Chapter 12

Gratitude

On the last day of July, I heave my four-foot luggage bag, a sleeping bag and my bright yellow twenty-litre waterproof backpack from the side of a big blue bus. I'm two hundred and fifty kilometres north of Toronto, yet the sun glares down on my exposed neck in the Huntsville heat.

After donning the backpack, I try wrapping one arm around the thick sleeping bag. I only manage a slowly slipping hold. I stand my luggage bag upright and drag its wheels over the uneven, woodchip-laden hill and look for my cabin.

As a Leadership Development Participant, an LDP, I suppose most would know their cabin. Most campers, I reckon, by the time they join LDP have probably attended Camp Huronda multiple times over multiple summers and know the lay of the land.

When I reach the hill, I spot a caravan of bussers lugging their bags together heading towards a series of cabins. The rustic cabins at Huronda are named after animals, like the beaver, the orca, the deer, the otter and so on. Dust, woodchips and mud cover the floor. It's different from Camp Discovery in London. At Discovery, cabins are named after trees, like the maple tree, the sycamore and the pine.

One by one each of the other diabetics split off from the small caravan and enter their respective cabins. We pass by the dining hall, the medical cabin and…shower and washroom cabins!?

I take a quick peek inside one of the two bathroom cabins and note the slightly muddy floor, the small mini-sinks, the solitary urinal and the three cramped toilet stalls. Each stall contains a poster, either immaturely drawn or professionally printed, of the seven different types of poop one can have…It's going to be a long twenty-seven days.

Two stall doors have broken locks. One of the toilets, which was too small for me, sits slightly loose in the floor. The urinal looks horrible.

At Camp Discovery, there aren't any woodchips and cabins have clean floors and clean showers and washrooms. Camp Discovery feels like a five-star hotel compared to Huronda.

Then again, Camp Discovery rents the property from Camp Woodeden, a camp for physically disabled children. And since when are camps supposed to feel like five-star hotels? Still…It's going to be a long twenty-seven days.

I leave the washroom cabin and join back up with the dwindling caravan of campers. Soon just two girls remain alongside me, one looks Asian with long brown hair and blonde highlights, the other girl a whiter, paler complexion dotted with freckles and dark brown hair.

We come across two small white shacks with a dusty wooden step, a small clothesline at the side and a set of layered doors, the outer one made of glass and the inner made of wood. A green LDP label marks both. The two girls head off to the one marked for girls and I head to the one marked for boys.

Inside, six small mattresses take up the cabin. Two bunkbeds line the wall while two single beds take up the middle, a small half-wall separating them. Multiple bedside tables sprawl either near the beds or walls.

The largest one, right next to the door, hosts a sharps container, a few bottles of dextrose sugar tablets, a few chewy bars, three containers for glucometer strips and a glucometer case with a fading name embossed on it.

Large names plainly decorate sheets of paper stuck to the sides of beds, one for each camper, briefly mentioning whether the camper is a pumper using an insulin pump, or an injector using insulin needles. I use a pump. So does everyone else except Benjamin, our counsellor. His tag doesn't specify injector or pumper.

A wooden change room stands in the corner opposite the door in front of my bunkbed. It's seems like the only semblance of privacy in the cabin. The ceiling shows the wooden beams and two-by-fours holding the small shack in place. Bits of graffiti and vandalism mark the beams and the undersides of the beds as well, showing "Jeff was here! '08!" and the like. Surprisingly, no swear words mar the cabin walls.

"Hey, who're you?" a voice with an Irish-accent asks me. I turn and see a white boy standing by the door, clad in brown shorts, a white sweat-soaked T-shirt and a p-cap with bits of short sandy hair peeking through. Most noticeably of all are the rope bracelets that adorn his wrist, a swath of colors making one bracelet hard to distinguish from the next.

"Uh, Abd-Abdullah," I say, somehow managing to stutter over my own name. It's a common enough name in Mississauga and Toronto where there are more Muslims. However, three hundred kilometres up north and I don't want someone to mispronounce a name they probably haven't heard before.

"Abdullah? That name rings a bell…" The boy rolls the name around his tongue. "Hey, you wouldn't happen to be the same Abdullah who was supposed to be a part of C-Sesh last year, would ye?"

C-Sesh as in C-Session, the first two weeks of August dedicated to the third Huronda Camp session.

"Ah, yeah, I was, but my family plans shifted. I was halfway across the world when C-Sesh started."

Last year was supposed to be my first time at Huronda, except my family made last-minute plans for a six-week vacation back home in Pakistan instead.

At the time, I didn't know whether I wanted to be with my extended family for six weeks or essentially with strangers sharing an incurable disease for two weeks. After the family vacation, however, where everyone remained a couch potato, I knew I missed out. I hoped to make up for it. The Leadership Development Program extended over C-session and into D-session—twenty-seven days.

"Oh, that's makes sense," he says. "My name's Aiden, by the way. Hey, Jamie!" Aiden turns around and yells out the doorway as another boy, with wavy light brown hair, creamy skin and blue eyes, strolls into the cabin. "This is the guy from last year, ye know the one that never showed up?"

"Ah, I see. Sup', my dude? How you doing?" The drawled-out tone is a real contrast to Aiden's faster Irish tone. "I'm Jamie."

"Nice to meet you, I'm Ab-Abdullah." Again!

"Anyways, you should probably start getting ready, mate," Aiden says to me as he pulls clothes out of a bag. "We have our swim test right now and we better not be late for that."

"Thanks for the notice, I appreciate it," I mutter and turn to my own unopened bag to look for my swimming shorts and T-shirt.

The swim test should be easy enough. I just need to swim twenty-five metres twice, then tread water for a short sixty seconds, and voila. It should be just a little harder than wading through water, I imagine.

Gratitude

Nothing to it.

It will probably be more of a challenge living a month among dirty washrooms and cramped wooden cabins that look like they were built decades ago. Never mind the million mosquitos that made Huronda their permanent breeding ground.

I miss the dirty washrooms and cramped wooden cabins that look like they were built decades ago. I miss the million mosquitos that made Huronda their permanent breeding ground. At least at Huronda, mosquitos were the only thing we had to worry about as we lay on soft beds in warm wooden cabins near washrooms with running water and showers that… just existed.

As I shift around in the four-man tent in our first wilderness trip night in Algonquin Park, my thigh groans in protest against the wide rock jutting into it. The tent was set near the edge of a small, rocky and very hilly island. A thin waterproof tarp remains the only barrier between our tents and the drizzle or downpour of a rainstorm. Ugh! The rock's too wide to curve my legs around. And a rock seems to be rubbing by my armpits. I try and curl myself into the least uncomfortable position and settle my head onto my makeshift pillow—my eternally damp towel scrunched into a plastic bag.

With a dozen sixty-litre barrels and tent and sleeping bags to carry, no one could bring anything as big as a full-size pillow. Hence the makeshift pillow. The towel never dries—at camp it's either damp from me drying myself after the daily swim session or drenched by an unexpected downpour whenever I hang it outside on the clothesline to dry.

After about eleven days or so of camp, a permanent stench has buried itself into the fabric—one of Waseosa Lake water, campground woodchips and the mass of sweat collected from my overactive body.

And I sleep with this stench now.

Not that the others probably noticed—everyone stinks after a day of canoeing, portaging and drenching themselves in the rain—and over the course of the next four days no one will be taking a shower anyway.

Somehow, the other three boys in the tent sleep soundly.

"...and you said that te..." Aiden sleep talks. Jamie lightly snores away next to him. On my other side, Hayden sleeps silently and motionless. They've all been on wilderness trips in past years and it seems they have learned to sleep like this. I don't have that luxury.

"...shot an ace toda..." Aiden continues to mutter. Just what is he dreaming about?

Poop?

Earlier that day…

"Yo, Jamie just shot an Ace right now, heh," Aiden chuckles as he comes back to the damp fireplace. It's not raining as hard as before when our tripper, Mike, took control of the group and ordered an immediate landing at the nearest campsite—one that happened to be God's hilliest and rockiest creation in all of Algonquin Park.

Right now, the rain drizzles intermittently. Not that it matters, though. The wood needed for a fire remains damp from the earlier downpour. Steep hills dominate the miniature island.

"Woah, man, an Ace off the bat? Hot Damn!" Jamie says and fist bumps Aiden. Apparently, shooting an ace is a feat of some kind?

"Hey, what's an Ace?" I ask. They can't be talking about shooting a gun. This is Canada not America!

"A clean dump, mate," Jamie replies. "No need to wipe with toilet paper cuz there's nothing left."

Wait…what?!

Gratitude

"Of course, you don't need to do an Ace-in-the-hole," Jamie says. "I just happened to find an opportunity on the cliff on the other side of the island. Too bad there ain't no trees to hang off from and do a Flying Dutchman."

Do I want to know what a "Flying Dutchman" is?

"But you can always use the thunder box…"

Why do I need to go now that he mentioned it?

"Gotta go there right now, actually," I say. "I'll see y'all in a bit. And nobody better come my way, 'kay?!"

I grab the toilet paper role from Aiden and sprint towards the hillside path leading to the thunder box. I look around and see no one. Good.

Sitting in the junction between the two parts of the camp, the thunder box remained standing over what seemed like a year of solid use. A wet wooden lid protects the seating area with a tiny hole showing the wooden cavity. Damp moss sticks to the side and a stench of wet rotting wood, mixed in with the poop, pee and toilet paper of the thousand people before me, invades my nostrils.

"Remember to be careful, Abdullah," Hayden warned me earlier. "Some mosquitos can land right on your privates if you're not careful. Happened to me once. Worst bite ever!"

I constantly check my surroundings, for both humans and insects, and perform a half-squat, half-stand over the thunder box hole. No way I want to be bitten by some hidden insect on my privates!

I finish up and head to where everyone gathers more firewood. I have no idea how such damp wood will catch fire.

"Glad we came to Algonquin instead of the other park that I can't remember the name of, that one doesn't even have thunder boxes," Aiden tells the other boys when I arrive.

So even built wooden boxes for doing your business are a luxury? The camp bathrooms seemed bad before but at least they were indoors with privacy and clean and had running water!

I walk past Aiden to look for more firewood for the fire. A single solitary quote by Mahatma Gandhi keeps reverberating through my head.

"I cried because I had no shoes, then I met a man who had no feet."

Chapter 13
Half-Drowned

"Alright, LDPs, no more endurance swims for the day," Jazz proclaims standing up high on the dock. Eight sore diabetics sputter to a stop along their swimming lanes.

I look on from my chair on the dock, clad in my damp blue bathrobe. Hayden, Aiden, Jade and Gem, closest to the dock, begin swimming back, the first three weaving through slow, sustained breaststrokes, the last scooping out an exhausted backstroke.

"No more endurance swims, but we still need to go over the theory and practice for rescuing victims out of the water, which you can all explain and do while treading water!" Jazz grins. Everyone else groans with weak protests.

"Abdullah, are you feeling better? Or do you still feel low?" asks Becka, the long blonde-haired lifeguard. Her freckled face scans mine before skimming over the bottle of half-empty dex tabs.

"Yes, I think I should be okay now," I mutter. I stand up from the damp foldable chair on the dock, shrug off my wet bathrobe, drop my glasses on the chair and tighten my goggles over the now-familiar stretchmarks etched on my visage. The constant wind creeps through my wet T-shirt. A shiver crawls down my spine. I hate it when that happens. It's like a snake wriggling up my back and sliding right by my heart.

The bottle of orange-flavoured dextrose tablets lies by the chair half-empty, a container of powdered sweetness reserved for the low blood sugars all campers experience a few million times over. The other half-a-container's worth of tablets lie dissolving in my stomach.

The doctors say the multiple lows are from increased physical activity and that makes sense given that we start the day at eight in the morning and run around camp for the next twelve hours instead of wasting time away in front of a computer screen.

The doctors also say to eat twenty-five more carbohydrates than what we give insulin for if we have a two-hour swimming session after dinner. If the past few years at camp can attest to anything, it's that whether you jump into a pool or a lake, for whatever reason, the act of swimming will almost inevitably pull your blood sugar levels like a whirlpool pulls down a ship.

Low blood sugar levels are bad—as in can-cause-seizure-coma-and-death-fast-if-left-untreated bad. Running blood sugars too high isn't good, either. However, whereas normal blood sugar levels remain around 5.0-9.0 millimolar for diabetics, a high or hyperglycaemic reading usually starts at 14.0 millimolar. Adults are considered impaired if they drive over a reading of 19.0 millimolar. Nerves can die at readings of 55. Death can also eventually occur after days of neglect. Such neglect is rare.

By contrast, where 5.0 millimolar is considered normal, anything lower than 3.9 millimolar is considered low or hypoglycaemic. Anything lower than 3.0 is worse. People can faint at the 2.0 mark. Blood glucometers usually can't measure below 1.1 millimolar. To hit absolute 0... given that the brain runs entirely on sugar, 0 can be fatal.

At camp, I usually hit 2.4 millimolar without realizing it. Like right now.

Logically, by eating more food and giving less insulin, diabetic blood sugars will run slightly higher after mealtime. Relatively speaking, running slightly higher with the high chance of dropping down to normal levels is definitely better than the alternative.

Me, being stupid ol' me, didn't this time. I should have, but I didn't. I'm not good at swimming. I've gotten better but I'm still nowhere near bronze. But if I didn't need to do as strenuous activities as the rest of the LDPs, surely I wouldn't need to make this extra calculation, right?

Right?

"Whenever you're ready, Abdullah! And remember to push down right when you hit the water!" Becka shouts as she jumps into the freezing Waseosa waters.

Right.

Push down.

With my hands.

I bend down. I just need to jump into the water. Whatever happens, I'll be fine. Becka's right there and Jazz is five feet away. My body doesn't feel low anymore. It was so much easier a few days ago.

To jump.

The sky was cloudy on the first afternoon of the new camp session. A slight wind, pleasant for most campers, constantly wheezed its way through. The day wasn't as glaringly hot and humid as it was a few hours ago in the morning.

For most campers, the slightly cool temperature helped integrate them into the camp life of the next two weeks. For those who waited until the afternoon for their swim test, however, the wind chilled their bones out on the lake edge.

"Come on, folks!" someone yelled from the waterfront.

No one moved. I leaned closer to the edge of the dock. One girl shivered as a brisk wind once again swished through the clouded summer afternoon. It's summer—but summer in Huntsville in August doesn't seem ideal for swimming, especially when compared to Mississauga, three hundred kilometres to the south.

"What are you waiting for!?" A slight impatience resonated throughout the nine Leadership Development Participants shuffling on the dock. The dock started to tip slightly—like a ship about to capsize.

"Jump!" yelled Jazz the Waterfront head. She would've been quieter with a megaphone. "We don't have all day!" In quick succession Jamie jumped, then Aidan, and after quickly securing my swimming goggles one last time, I jumped straight into the frigid water.

Shit! The water in this part of the lake is much deeper than any pool I ever swam in. I needed to rise back up to the surface. There was less than a metre of water between me and the surface.

I barely made it.

Anyone looking from the Big Steps above—a bunch of benches at the side of the hill facing the waterfront—would've see nine campers jump in the water in quick succession but only eight surface to start their twenty-five metre swim test. The last one, me, they would've seen a chaotic splash zone and a flurry of limbs making sure the owner of said limbs could stay alive.

Alright, Abdullah, focus! I told myself. *You just have to swim three metres back to the start of the lane, then swim the twenty-five metres forward and back and then tread water for a minute. It can't be that hard!*

I gasped and heaved in a bit of air. It didn't feel like enough. I gasped again. Some water slipped in.

Just get into a back float! You know how to do that! Just back float your way through the swim test!

I arched my back and puffed out my chest. My feet couldn't come nearly up enough. I continued to sink. My hands started to flail. I needed to stay afloat! I briefly caught sight of the floatation tube held at the ready by Jazz's feet on the dock. "Hey! Are you okay? Can you—"

"I'm fine!" I spurted and finally reached the start of the lane. Everyone else was already on the other side making their way back. I started my flailing drowning doggy paddle across the lane.

Crap. How the hell am I supposed to go all the way through the lane and back?

Perhaps a tad bit late, I realized, I was clearly not fine.

"Help—" I sank below the water but broke through the surface once more, and in a panic, I almost missed the float held by a rope Jazz threw towards me. I wrapped my arms around it in a bear hug.

Stupid, Abdullah! What were you even thinking?

As I jump into the water beside Becka, I catch sight of the plastic paper bracelet wrapped around my right wrist. All campers must go through a swim test that determines whether they need a life jacket when swimming.

A red bracelet shows you passed the test. A yellow bracelet with the word RED spelled out in permanent marker shows you passed the test, later on or that the camp was running out of bracelets. A plain yellow bracelet says you need a life jacket when in the water.

Of the nine LDPs, I'm the only one starting university in the fall. The rest haven't graduated high school yet. I am younger than my counsellors by two years, but in the entire camp, I am either a year older than half the staff or the same age as them.

I am one of a handful of campers who don a plain yellow bracelet and the others are ten years younger than me.

The water reaches out to grab me. My hands splash down just enough to pull my head and shoulders out of the water.

Alright, Abdullah, just tread, keep on treading, come on, you can do this. This mantra churns through my mind. I zone everything else out. Only my mantra, my breath and my constantly moving arms and legs stay on repeat. Somehow, I do not lose control.

"Can we all just pause," Jazz intones to the other LDPs, "and give a huge shout out to Abdullah who has managed to tread water for two whole minutes!"

What?

"Woohoo! Go, Abdullah!" Vic shouts.

"Proud of ye, mate!" Aiden yells.

The bellow of approval and encouragement more than suffices for the lack of applause—treading water for ten minutes is hard enough. Swimming without worry?

That would be amazing

Chapter 14

Rage Room

Crack! Crack! Crack! Thud!

Anyone who passed by the campsite at the end of North Tea Lake probably heard the sound of wood smashing on rock—frequently. They would have also been surprised at the cheers emanating near the dead campfire, cheers from eight LDPs—Hayden, Aidan, Jamie, Renee, Gem, Jen, Jade and Vic—and counsellors Megan and Ben and field nurse Will.

The sun shines for the first time on the afternoon of our second day on our five-day wilderness trip in Algonquin Park. For the moment, it's a welcome change from the constant downpours of yesterday and provides an opportunity to collect dry firewood for our campfire.

In the case of this specific campsite, however, most of the firewood lies near a pre-made hearth of boulders and stone. The firewood comes in the form of smooth, cylindrical logs as long as our arms and as wide as our heads and needs to be broken down into smaller pieces to burn more easily.

"Hyaa!" My yell pierces the mid-day lull of the national park.

The problem is our head tripper, Mike, currently asleep in his tent despite the ruckus, did not bring an axe from Camp Huronda.

Despite being the oldest at seventeen among a group of mostly fifteen- and sixteen-year-olds, the excursion marks my first wilderness trip. Despite being a novice, I seem to rock enough to throw a spectacle for a crowd of diabetics and try to break some much-needed wood at the same time.

"Hyaa!" Breaking sturdy logs with one's bare hands would be easy if I were, say, the Hulk. Unfortunately, I am not.

Bumpy balsam bark rotates roughly along my hands, not enough to bruise, but enough to feel uncomfortable. My grip remains loose against the still intact log. Wider than I can grasp and shorter than my arm, my two-handed grip fails to encompass the unbroken piece of wood.

Smash!

Not that I mind too much. A looser hold allows for larger recoil from the angled rock slab protruding from the flat ground. Shrapnel-like bits fling out from the bark, lodging into my dark blue, waterlogged windbreaker. The log ricochets back to me, stopping two inches in front of my face every time I smash it on the slab.

I don't care. My pupils dilate. My veins bulge. Adrenaline surges through my brain.

Still, the log remains unscathed.

"GIVE ME AN 'A'!"

"A! YOU GOT YOU'RE A, YOU GOT YOUR A!"

Leave it to Vic to start a cheer.

A grin ripples across my face. My heart pounds. I've never been the object of a cheer before. I feel a loose tendril of my shoe whip across my shin. I stop beating the log against the rock. My shoelace comes undone.

Silence stops the cheer. I drop the log and bend down. Everyone else seems confused.

"Abdullah, are you alright?" yells my counsellor, Ben.

"Sorry, my shoe just came undone!"

I rush to tie the knot. It's harder to do with a wet pair of shoes soaked from canoeing. I want to get back to beating the log. The camp needs firewood. I want to keep this spectacle going.

I pick up the log again and glance at the trees surrounding me. One stands out near Ben's GoPro camera that's recording the entire event. The tree stands on a slight decline, separate from the other trees and thinner than the rest.

I take the log in both hands, grip the two ends, and hold it flat in front of my shoulders. My feet dig into the ground, like the super-powered heroes in TV shows. For them, their firm feet flex, the ground splits open beneath, they rush forward like a wild, angry bull, and smash their nemesis into a billion pieces. They always come out victorious.

For me, my soaked shoes squeak. I rush forward like a ragged dog. My arch nemesis, the inanimate log, makes a soft thud against the unimposing bark of the thin tree. My shoelace comes undone.

"S-U-P-E-R! SUPER, SUPER THAT'S WHAT YOU ARE!"

My frown changes back into a grin—everyone still cheers for me! I won't give up! I tie my shoelace again. I readjust the unbroken piece of wood in my hands and exaggerate a lumbered step across the flat clearing. One of my steps turns me towards the stack of laid red canoes.

"Abdullah, not there!" Megan shouts.

I dramatize a tripping side-step, my right leg shooting in front and across my left, before breaking out into a low, hunched-back stumble. I slam the log into the tree. Nothing. I slam it again and a small bit of bark falls off. I rotate, giving my arms a wide, clumsy arc, and then slam the log down onto the protruding rock. Larger yet still insignificant pieces fall away. I swing the log again and it slips out of my hand.

My shoelace comes undone. Again.

My audience lets out a collective gasp. My hands sting. Slight bits of the topmost layer of bark have peeled away. Nothing serious. Yet I need to move along in my progress. My veins bulge. My heart pounds hard. I restrain my tongue from panting. My limbs shake slightly—whether from hypoglycemia or from adrenaline, I don't know and I don't care.

"Alright, no"—I gulp in a breath—"holding back!"

I shrug off my windbreaker and throw it over the log. My orange camp T-shirt soaked in sweat sticks to my skin. I grip the wrapped log and lumber again towards the tree, towards the rock, away from the boats, in my wet socks.

I go Super Saiyan with a maniac grin turned snarl. The tree shakes. Some leaves fall. Bits of bark fall off. I continue hitting the log against the tree. Bark bits now continuously explode out of the wood but still insignificant. My legs quiver. They can only lumber across the ground now. My shoelace comes undone, again.

"R-O-C-K! YOU ROCK, YOU ROCK! R-O-C-K! YOU ROCK, YOU ROCK!"

Another cheer erupts. Amazing! How long can they keep this up? They must be tired.

I kneel and tie my shoelace for the umpteenth time. I glance at the still dead firepit a few metres away, a hollow surrounded by an assortment of stones. I look at the stones again. They're dense enough to crack a skull if someone fell on them by mistake. A skull is much denser than wood, right?

I drag the still intact piece of log towards the firepit. I spot two flat stones near the top of the hollow. I remove them and place the two stones shoulder-width apart. I balance the log on the two stones and make sure it's suspended off the ground.

I look back at the hollow and spot another, much larger, rock, fat but with a slight edge on one side. Perfect. I bend down and heave it out of the side of the hollow, freeing it from the base, and then lift it chest height, the edge perpendicular to the forever-damned log.

The crowd withholds their cheers and stays silent. Sweat drips down my drenched shirt. Over the top of the huge rock, I glare at the tattered log. Bits of bark have come off in places but the shape remained unbroken. My legs quiver as I raise the rock up to shoulder height. I swing down.

Crack! Nothing.

Crack! Nothing.

Crack! Again!

Multiple lines run through the log and billions of bark bits line the ground and yet the log stays unbroken. I raise the stone high above my head, as if reaching for the heavens and swing down the guillotine.

Die you unholy piece of shit!

The log finally breaks.

"WE ARE PROUD OF YOU! SAY WE ARE PROUD OF YOU SAY WHAT? WE ARE PROUD OF YOU, SAY WE ARE PROUD OF YOU SAY HEY!"

Wood chips stick to my buckled knees. My thighs quiver. My mouth gasps. My heart pumps—furiously. I slump onto the ground, my legs now sprawled in front of me.

"Hey, Will? I think I'm going low…"

The nurse rushes towards me with glucose tablets in one hand and a glucose meter in the other hand. Ben collects his GoPro and checks the recording time. He gawks.

"Forty minutes!?!"

Chapter 15
Time To Go

"That's it, Abu, another arm raise! And another! Keep going. You're doing great!" Mama says to Dada from across the TV lounge. My grandfather stands near the sofa, hands off his walker in front of him, back as straight as possible. I stand by in case he needs any help.

Dada couldn't move too well for the first few days after his surgery. He stayed in bed a lot. He slept a lot. When he walked, he had to hunch forward and use his walker. Whenever he used it, he tried to keep his back straight—eyes focused ahead, his breath steady and his dignity intact.

Dada raises his arm up and down fluently and rapidly. It's the last day of his visit. He arrived in May. It's now almost March.

When Dada gets out of bed each morning, he stretches his arms, yawns and combs back his hair. Then he starts to reach for his cane before stopping himself as if he just remembered that he can't use his cane anymore and reaches for his walker. He hates the walker. A permanent frown mars his face.

"Rabia, that's enough," Baba says as he comes down the stairs, his hair wet and slicked back after a shower. "Abu has his flight today. We don't want to tire him needlessly."

Dada's return flight to Pakistan is in three hours at seven p.m. He still needs to get out of his pyjamas, shower and put on his coat. It's a freezing February winter day in Canada.

"Alright, I'll take a shower in a bit," Dada says out of breath. "Just let me rest for a second."

He places his hands—reluctantly—on his walker and then hobbles over to the sofa. I clear the sofa of a blanket and misplaced cushions.

"Abdullah, can you get me some water?" Dada asks.

I nod and rush into the kitchen. I pull out a large, heavy glass and fill it halfway with cold fridge water and the other half with warmer tap water. I power walk my way back to Dada and present him the tall glass.

He glances down at his hands resting on his lap. They shake. I read Mama's eyes. *Idiot! Dada can't hold such a big glass, get a smaller one at once.*

"Uh, sorry Dada, I'll get you another gla—"

He snatches the glass from my hand. A slosh of water spills out. Dada draws the glass to his mouth, takes a gulp, then another, then another, then finishes it and hands it back to me. His hand shakes. A bead of sweat runs down his face. I take the glass back before it drops.

Dada leans back into the sofa. He smiles. His eyes relax. He takes in a deep breath. And out. His hand reaches out and rests on his cane. He doesn't get up. He stays there, sitting on the sofa, hand holding his cane.

"Abdullah, come here please!" I hear Baba call me from Dada's room. "Can you get this suitcase into the car?"

The bulging blue suitcase has a broken handle, one wheel grated out into more of a square block than a wheel, and a zipper that looks like it's about to pop off. "Property of Dr. Abdul-Rashid Sher" adorns the suitcase in black ink.

The suitcase is ancient. Dada probably used this same suitcase a million times by now. Not that Baba didn't try to replace it. I guess Dada just grew attached to it. Still, this will probably be its last trip.

I nod to Baba. I don't think he notices. He looks like he's about to collapse from exhaustion. The bags under his eyes seem darker. His fingers twitch. Despite all of this his eyes scan through a neck pouch, making sure Dada will have everything he needs to get through security at his fingertips.

I drag the suitcase from the den to the front door. I have to stop it a few times from falling over to one side because of the wheel. I don't understand Dada's attachment. Wouldn't it be better to just get rid of it? It would certainly make travelling a lot easier. I place the suitcase into the trunk and return to the TV lounge.

Dada sits still, breathing in and out, hand on his cane. It almost looks like he's sleeping. I sit next to him, close my eyes and match my breathing with his. Breathe in when he breathes in, breathe out when he does. His breath still stinks after all these years.

"Abdullah." Dada's voice breaks the silence. "What's the time?"

"Dada, it's almost four."

"Ah, alright."

Silence.

"What time is my flight again?"

"At seven, I think." Dada's flight previously got rescheduled after an airline strike messed up the schedule.

"Alright, thank you." Dada sits back in his seat. A small smile twitches at his lips.

Seconds later...

"So what time is it again?"

"What's going on?" Baba enters the TV lounge with Mama. His armpits sweat visibly.

Can someone help me figure out what's going on?

"Uh, Baba, um…" I gesture to Dada. Baba picks up the hint.

"Abu, is everything alright?" he asks.

"Yes, it is. Can you just tell me what time it is?"

"It's four, Abu." Baba raises his eyebrows. Dada is a doctor. A clock adorns the wall right in front of him. Maybe his vision is getting weak.

"So it's time for *Maghrib* (the sunset prayer), right?"

"Abu, Maghrib is at seven, we just told you it's four o'clock," Baba says with a rising voice.

"Yes, I know that. So, should we already be at the airport then?" Dada says and looks around, noticing his pyjamas.

"We will be leaving soon but first you have to change your clothes and take a shower."

"Ah, that makes sense," Dada says and nods in agreement. "So, it's seven o'clock right now?"

Baba grinds his molars. He closes his eyes. He takes a deep breath in. "I am sorry Abu, I cannot explain it to you right now. I…I need to be alone for a moment."

Baba's exit leaves Dada's question unanswered. Confusion remains sprawled over Dada's face. "Wait, but…what…where are you going?" He turns to me. "Abdullah." His voice shakes harder than his hands. His moist eyes stare into mine. "I'm going back to Pakistan today, right?"

I nod.

"What time is it again?"

"It's fou—" I cut myself off. "It's time to shower, Dada. You have a flight to catch."

"Okay."

Time To Go

He doesn't move.

We sit in silence for the last time.

When we part ways at the airport we take one final picture.

Dada is smiling.

In hindsight, months later when I looked back on his day of departure, I realize that day wasn't the first time Dada seemed confused.

It just happened to be the first time I saw it. In reality, Mama and Baba took him to the doctor days before his departure. The doctor assured them that Dada was simply homesick, having been away from Pakistan and from Dadi for over nine months. He assured them that Dada was fit to travel home alone. And a doctor would surely know the best course of action, right?

That same doctor was shocked when a few months later, Mama told him the correct diagnosis. I'm still dumbfounded to this day how the doctor missed something so major. Because while I can't confirm it, I'm pretty sure those were the days when it started.

Cancer.

Pictured from left to right:
My younger brother Hamza, Baba, Me, Dada (at the bottom) and Mama.

Chapter 16

God Willing

Fools' Day

In February 2016, when we dropped Dada off at the airport, despite the doctor's diagnosis, Baba still felt something was off. He repeatedly asked Dada to reconsider and abort the flight, and when Dada declined, Baba offered to accompany him on his return flight right then and there, extra costs be damned. Dada denied the need for any help.

In late March 2016, Baba rushes back to Pakistan. Dada is unwell, losing mobility, and constantly confused. When Baba arrives, he expects some sort of support system to be in place. The home does afterall house his older sister, her family, and a plethora of well-cared-for, well-paid servants.

He is wrong.

Baba returns to Canada with Dada after April Fool's Day.

One last secret

We admit Dada into the Trillium Health Partners Mississauga Hospital in mid-April. An oncologist diagnoses him with Stage 4 lung carcinoma—lung cancer. It went undetected throughout the five months Dada had previously been in the hospital.

Baba once had to stop the oncologist from revealing this information right in front of Dada.

This time, I don't ask why we must keep another secret.

Constant

Mama and Baba visit Dada every day. Hamza goes with them sometimes on weekends when he doesn't have too much homework.

I haven't been able to visit yet. Stupid exams.

Baba's sleep schedule has been ruined since he took care of Dada during his heart surgery months ago. Stress now compiles on top of his sleeplessness, like a nasty piece of compound interest. He sleeps at five in the morning and wakes up at two in the afternoon, then dozes again for thirty minutes in the day and faces insomnia during the next night again.

One day, I see my mother cooking in the kitchen. "What are you making, Mama?" I peer over her shoulder. In a steel pot rises a familiar white semisolid, bubbling in milk that clump into chunks before Mama methodically breaks them down again.

"I'm cooking kheer, rice pudding, for Dada," Mama says as her eyes stay focused on the pot. She dips a spoon in and scoops out a small sample. Jiggling the spoon around, she drips off some of the liquid.

"Your dada likes thick kheer with large grains of rice. Oh!" She gives a small gasp before taking out a jar of sugar. She lifts the lid off the top and fills it with sugar before dumping the lid into the pot.

Another dump of sugar. And another.

"Mama, isn't that a lot of sugar?"

"Dada likes his kheer sweet." Her eyes remain fixated on her pot. "The hospital food is very bland so he requested this...might as well give him the very best...."

Hair no more

Dada smacks his lips, scoops up the remaining rice pudding on his plate and peers into the bag next to him to see if there is more. One day the Pakistani political comedy show *Hasb-e-Haal* plays on the TV in front of him when I walk into the hospital room with Mama.

Baba stands by the doorway with Hamza, trying not to overcrowd the private hospital ward. According to Baba, Dada is more lucid today.

"Assalam-u-alikum, Dada."

He glances up from the TV screen.

"Abdullah!" He grins. "I haven't seen you in so long!"

"Sorry, Dada. I've been busy preparing for my IB exams." I plaster on a smile. "I would have visited earlier if I could. How is the kheer?"

I try to ignore his thinning arms and the urinary catheter snaking out from under his hospital gown.

"The kheer is amazing!" Dada responds. "Rabia, you did a fantastic job!"

"Oh thank you, Abu!" Mom beams. Her shoulders relax. "I'm glad you enjoyed it!"

"Abdullah, do you want some?" Dada asks. Half the bowl remains.

"Oh don't worry, Dada. I had some at home. You keep eating. The hospital food here sucks from what I've heard."

"It's tasteless!" Dada puckers his lips in disgust. "No spice at all!"

"Don't worry, Dada, Inshallah, you'll get out of here in n-no time at all. When we go back home, Mama can cook you all the biryani you want!"

"Abu," Mama interrupts. "I brought a comb. Why don't I brush your hair for you?"

"Sure. Thank you, Rabia, I forgot to do that for a while."

Dada's hair looks thinner but it's still long. Mama rifles her hand through it to remove any tangles. The fewer tangles, the less pain he might feel. Her hand softly pulls his hair from his forehead towards his scalp. Her hand comes off his head with a large clump of thin white hair.

Mama's eyes widen.

Baba steadies himself by the door.

Hamza's eyebrows shoot up.

My smile strains.

Dada doesn't seem to notice.

Mama looks down and, slowly, hoping it was just a fluke, caresses her hand through Dada's hair again. Another clump of sick grey hair falls on the backside of Dada's gown.

Walker

"Abdullah, come help me get Dada ready for his shower!" Mama calls from Dada's room. I rush over from the kitchen. My rice pudding will have to wait.

"What's going on?" Dada asks.

His confusion is common now.

"It's time for a shower, Abu," Mama intones.

"I don't feel like taking a shower right now," Dada says and turns his head away.

"Abu, you haven't taken a shower in three days," Mama responds. "You need to take a shower today." Dada now spends most of his days on a custom bed the hospital provided. A diaper stops major accidents from occuring. Baba changes it multiple times each day. He keeps Dada's bowel area as clean as possible, enduring the stink, making sure not to miss any folds in the skin where poop might stay lodged and fester. Mama helps. I suck at helping.

God Willing

Yet despite the care, without a shower at least once every three days, ulcers and infections remain a constant threat.

"I will take one later." Dada doesn't realize it. Not that he can understand much these days.

I've been told that Dada listens to me. I take my shot. "Dada, please, it'll only take like five minutes and then you'll be clean and fresh!"

"Abdullah, I'm tired, I will take it—"

"Please, Dada?"

"Oh, alright."

Hamza and I help Dada stand up. I reach for his walker, position it in front of him and then grab him by his armpit. Hamza gets under his other one. For the next five minutes, we labour through the four-metre walk to the washroom where Baba waits.

Dada doesn't mind the walker now. He still looks to his cane at times but knows he can no longer use it. He can barely use his walker, even when Hamza and I help him. His back hunches over. He no longer tries to keep it straight. He no longer has the energy.

In the powder room, beside the toilet, is a Muslim shower, a bidet, which acts like a mini-hose and jets out water. Dada, stripped by Baba, sits down on the toilet seat. I look away. I'm supposed to become a doctor yet I can't face a naked body. As the washroom door closes, the cries from inside vibrate throughout the entire house.

"Haroon! Stop it!" Dada yells. "It's too hot! It's coming too fast! Stop it!" It's not that the shower is too hot or too fast, nor too cold or too slow. Baba tests both temperature and pressure multiple times before each bath to make sure the shower remains gentle and warm.

Dada just isn't in a right state of mind.

"Just a little bit longer, Abu, it won't be long now!" Baba yells over the water and rushes through the bath.

"Haroon! Stop it! Stop it! Don't do it, don't do it!"

"I'm almost done Abu. Just hold on for one more minute! Please!"

I want to shut my ears and go upstairs. I want to go study for the exam I didn't want to study for before.

After the bath, Baba dresses Dada in loose clean pyjamas before stumbling his way to the TV lounge. Tears streak down his face. Mama and I drag Dada back to his bed. He falls asleep. Mama then goes to take care of Baba in the TV lounge.

I head back upstairs. I don't need to hear anymore sobbing right now.

Sleep

On June 12, 2016, I sneak past Dada's room at midnight for a small snack. He snores. I can hear him from upstairs. I enter the kitchen and spy a large empty blue bowl sitting on the counter. Clumps of rice pudding lie at the bottom. I take a small teaspoon and gather the last few chunks and devour them.

Delicious. Finished.

Dada's snores become louder. On my way to the stairs, I sneak up to the double doorway, dip my head through the opening and glance inside, just to make sure he's sleeping alright. Dada snores with his mouth open. With his hands by his side. Eyes wide open.

We make eye contact for a second. I spy a white film-like substance covering the back of his mouth. A fungal infection. He heaves through a breath. His eyes glisten. My eyes bolt. I close the crack in the door. I speed walk up to my room. I briefly hear Baba's hiccuped inhales and strained exhales in the room next door.

I try to fall asleep but every time I close my eyes, I drift back to the man downstairs who snores but cannot sleep and his son upstairs who heaves but cannot breathe.

In Islam, the concept of euthanasia, of mercy killing, of purposefully ending one's life to relieve suffering, is forbidden because only God can give life, and only God can take it away.

God takes Dada's life two days later.

"Come home by Uber. Dada isn't doing too well," Mama texts me after school.

When I reach home a nurse stands near the edge of the room, packing up equipment the hospital lent us, including the bowl of morphine injections. Mama sobs. The new Sher family patriarch shuts down.

Doctors had estimated another six months. Baba was more than prepared to take care of him. He also knew death was inevitable. Still. When you expect another six months with your father and lose him six days later instead, life suddenly feels a bit too empty. A white sheet covers the body. A white ribbon is messily tied around his head, framing closed eyes and stoic lips, and obscuring the thin, clumpy and easily removable patches of hay-like hair.

"Mama—"

"It happened just...minutes ago," Mama sobs out. "He couldn't speak but..." She looks to Baba. He looks back. "...we started saying the *Qalima* beside him and his...his tongue was moving, like it was trying to imitate us." A small smile breaks through between her tears.

The Qalima, the Islamic oath that witnesses that there is but one God and the Prophet Muhammad is his messenger, is what people say when they become Muslim. It's also what Muslims believe should be said at the time of death to increase one's favour with God and achieve greater success in the afterlife.

I smile back. "Inshallah then, he is in *Jannah* (paradise)."

I don't say it out loud.

But.

I'm glad my grandfather is dead.

Chapter 17
Transient Means Fleeting

Transient means "fleeting." Specifically, in relation to time, an object or an event that only lasts for but a moment. It's impermanent. Contrast the length of a human life with the cosmos. Or perhaps the jolt of pain a needle delivers when it pricks the skin. It's only temporary.

"Fleeting" also applies to the feet fleeing to the finish line—away from us. The runners, their transient footsteps touching the ground for a mere instant, and then move onwards through the course.

Transient does not, however, apply to us.

For fleeting also gives a sense of urgency, I suppose, a sense of excitement, a sense of…anything but my current job. I'm a volunteer at the Toronto Colour Run. I always imagine spraying the runners with coloured powder or working somewhere near the chaotic mini-concert happening in the vicinity.

The Woodbine Centre Parking lot is large and empty for a part of the day. The concert screams contentment and joy. Music blares and people dance—well, flail wildly—while spraying coloured powder from the multiple disposable packets handed out around the event.

Every so often, a plethora of coloured madness emanates from the crowd, an explosion of colour as the band hits an epic portion of whatever song they might be playing.

Yet amid the participants enjoying the different events of the colour run, volunteers spray participants as they run and manage the sound system for the concert, we, as in me and one other person, set up twelve-foot flags at the start line.

The task starts and ends laboriously. We open flag bags, we insert disassembled rods into one another, we put the flag on like a sock on a misshapen foot, we insert the flag into its holding along the side of the track and we reinsert flags taken away by the wind. Repeat.

Our supervisor lazes on her high wooden chair fifteen feet above the ground, an umbrella propped open on one side to shield her from the sun, a phone in one hand and a glass of lemonade in her other hand.

You could help us out, you know! I glare my thoughts at her from the corner of my eye as I finish another flag. Not that my glaring thoughts would actually reach her with her face glued to her phone. Armageddon could happen and she might not notice. What a pathetic role model.

While some "volunteers" help by doing absolutely nothing, chilling and hanging out, we oversee the start line, now outfitted with at least a hundred flags on each side. We hold a small, insignificant piece of tape to separate the waves of people itching to start the run.

"Move back, please!" I exclaim as another group of friends try to limbo under the tape we hold, trying to join friends who went on ahead.

Impatient pieces of...

I stop that train of thought.

Just relax, Abdullah, they are just participants with an abundant amount of energy. It's nothing to make a fuss over.

"Hey, hurry up! Let us through, man!" a man yells. *Ugh!*

"All you need to do is fold these flags," the supervisor monotones. "And roll these carpets here and then you can come ask for the next set of instructions." She sighs. A glance at her wristwatch turns the sigh into a slump.

My pity does not reach her.

Straighten up, you lazy piece of shit! What right do you have to complain, you did absolutely nothing ALL morning!

A sigh escapes from my partner, a man who suffered through the same menial tasks with me, and who shared a small laugh with me the day before the run started, who…not that it matters. I probably won't see him again after today. He will move on with his life and I with mine. He will become a fleeting memory in my mind—transient.

I groan as I turn my attention to the task at hand. Numerous times over the last hour I questioned why I volunteered for this event. It only lasts from six in the morning to two in the afternoon. With only two hours remaining, the runners have cleared the track a while ago and now watch the mini-concert, the climactic finale to the event.

Even from this distance, muffled by the numerous trucks, the craze from the fanatic ending washes over everyone in the vicinity. Everyone, volunteers and supervisors, quickly finishes their inconsequential jobs and shuffles to the concert—everyone, that is, except us.

Our supervisor downplayed the tediousness of our task. More than two hundred big flags lay on the ground, awaiting dismantlement, one at a time. The "carpet," stiff and heavy, lies one hundred metres long. I groan. Again. Damnit!

The bright bus doors open. The yellow paint on the bus glows, as if the Magic School Bus stood in front of us and not just another ordinary school bus taking a bunch of ordinary but colourful volunteers away from a vacant parking lot.

At two in the afternoon, the sun manages to partly hide behind clouds. Some volunteers exchange phone numbers. Others hoard packets of powdered colour, including me.

However, if a person happened upon the parking lot now, the only signs that an event known as the "Colour Run" ever happened might be the few splotches of colour on the ground—transient. Even those will have washed away in a few days.

As I board the bus, a few volunteers catch my gaze. Completely powdered in aquatic green mixed with a tinge of blue and hair crusted in pink, they almost look like the blue aliens from *Avatar*. In comparison, a faint streak of yellow on my dark blue pants and some flakes of red in my hair show up as the only stains on my person.

I reach the concert in its final stages when all the coloured powder lay in either people's hair or clothes or on the ground in a rainbow of pink, green, yellow, blue and purple.

Why did I come so late? Not to enjoy the show! My supervisor gave me the wondrous job of picking up garbage, colour packets and water bottles. I suppose supervisors assigned other volunteers as well—but obviously, I got the single garbage bag they possessed.

Yay me.

I feel exhausted as I slump in my seat and look out the window. The Colour Run finished for another year. It started at six. People came at eight or nine. The event wrapped up by one. The crew was packed up thirty minutes later.

Now it looks like it never existed.

Perhaps that statement holds some truth.
Yet the Colour Run existed.
And I for some reason volunteered for it.
And my supervisor assigned me the most menial jobs.
And now, it's over.
It feels…useless.
Wasteful.
Two in the afternoon and the Colour Run fled the scene.
I suppose it's like a runner's footsteps—the Colour Run is transient.
Transient means fleeting.

Chapter 18:
Second Family

Family: A noun used to describe a group made up of parents and children in a household, according to Google. Right below this first definition, family consists of "all the descendants of a common ancestor." The two definitions may sound the same because most families have a few generations connected via parent-child blood relations, and as such the children have the same common ancestor—the mother or father. One can even specify the type of family. For example, the traditional nuclear family of the 1950s became the flagship family of the era, with a breadwinner father, a stay-at-home mother and two, maybe three, happy children.

So then what do you call a group of high school students living together at a camp for a month with nothing in common except an incurable disease that, though people say advancements have been made towards a cure, you get the sinking feeling that a cure will be found only as soon as people take climate change seriously?

Conventionally, I suppose that doesn't constitute a family.

Meh. Who cares about conventional definitions in the twenty-first century?

Family: One of the few things a camper leaves behind for the one, two or four weeks they attend camp, besides things like personal electronic devices, late nights and lazy good mornings.

A camper leaves it behind for high ropes and to capture the flag, for pottery, arts and crafts, for archery and Frisbee, and for wilderness trips and Olympic-styled Concordia Days.

Technology becomes limited to the MP3 devices counsellors carry, and the laptop, radio and disc music put on during meals, and the many medical pumps and glucometers campers carry.

During the time campers stay at camp, the world downsizes to the one hundred and forty or so campers, camp staff, medical teams and the huskies and golden Labrador staff pets most campers adore.

New music, new movies, new deaths, new tragedies, new miracles, new discoveries, anything can happen outside the bubble and no camper would know unless the staff shared it—or if a camper received mail.

For two weeks, the world downsizes from seven billion to one hundred and forty—and for the Leadership Development Participants staying for a month, to less than seventy, nine LDPs, two counsellors and the rest of the camp staff.

Mail: The one way to communicate with the outside world—short of direct telephone service—not that anyone uses that option unless in an extreme emergency.

I remember before I went to the five-day Camp Discovery sessions, mail was stupid. Any mail received from parents, families and friends took at least two days and outgoing mail took a week. My parents still wanted me to send mail for some reason.

I didn't mail anything the first year I attended camp. The next year, it took two weeks to receive, by which time I had already returned home. The third year, I didn't bother.

Now here I sit, among friends who, surprisingly, use the ZAP (Zero Activity Program) Hour to write home instead of playing the Risk board game I brought to camp. My folks probably don't expect a letter. I don't have any postcards or stamps to begin with. I bet I can borrow some from my friends.

Mail: Evidently an invention wherein people seamlessly weave onion slices into the paper envelope. The first time people received mail at the LDP table during dinner, the recipients, Jade and Renee, caused mini-floods of salt-filled tears as they blubbered incoherent happiness.

I eventually receive a letter—emailed to camp by my brother Hamza using my personal laptop as he so cheekily pointed out. "I was surprised that you even wrote to us. I was not expecting that at all…when we received your letter, Mama started crying for some weird reason."

My unwatering eyes water slightly and my mouth curls into a perpetual grin for the rest of the night.

Family: A group you want to love but also tease constantly; who you want to tease constantly, but never hurt; who, if you do hurt them, or think you've hurt them, you feel like shit. That's probably what Vic, Jen and Aiden thought one night on our wilderness trip after they jumped on counsellor Benji's emerald green hammock and the one, max two-person hammock tore underneath them.

Cue the collective "Oh shit" moment.

Yet Ben didn't get angry but sad, and even that was overshadowed by his concern for Jen. She landed on a large pointy boulder stationed underneath the hammock. Later Jen, Aiden and Vic laid on flat rocks by the water's edge and muttered about how bad they felt and promised to pool in and buy Benji a new hammock.

At some point amid the muttered sorrow, Hayden joined them. When the hammock fell, he sat hidden in the dark, unnoticed by everyone.

Hayden wore a playful smile most of the day. He helped me integrate into camp when I first arrived. He accompanied me to the washroom most times of the day under the buddy system.

Hayden, who partnered with me in most initiatives, and who tolerated me through my many mistakes—now seemed lost in thought and not at all in a wistful or melancholic way. He seemed even sadder.

"Hayden you okay, man?" I ask after everyone left for the rocks by the water's edge, and again when we moved to the dying campfire near the rocks by the water's edge.

"It's nothing, Abdullah. I don't feel like talking about it."

"I'll be here if you do want to talk," I tell him.

Somehow I found myself sitting on the rocks accompanying the three guilt-ridden, hammock-destroyers and one mystery brooder through an hour of stargazing. Guilt didn't plague my conscience. So why was I there? I suppose I had become the eldest brother to thirteen others.

The joke hazing over the group of us was that Vic was referred to as the "Mom" of the group and me the "Dad."

Family: A vague term that can evidently mean anything from a group of people connected by marital relations and direct bloodlines to a group of people of varying backgrounds, religions and races connected through a deadly disease.

Diabetes isn't a diagnosis to celebrate. It's a disease that can complicate childhood health and cause serious effects in late adulthood. Left uncontrolled, it can rot a person physically and mentally like it did before insulin was discovered and synthesized.

While not as dangerous as something like cancer in the twenty-first century as it was in the early twentieth century and before when insulin wasn't discovered, diabetes is certainly more permanent.

While cancer patients and other victims of serious diseases sometimes recover completely and can live a cancer-free life, no one can say to a diabetic, "Don't worry, you'll be able to live a diabetes-free life tomorrow."

Diabetes is a harmful disease and not fully understood by nondiabetics. It is my fervent hope that after reading this collection of stories, one has learned more than they knew before.

Despite all the dilemmas and disasters diabetes brings, however, I know in hindsight that if I was ever given a choice to go back and alter the fabric of space-time somehow and stop myself from getting diabetes, I would not. I would not take back my diabetes if I could because then I would not have met this community connected beyond blood.

Diabetes is incurable, sure, but that doesn't mean one can't live a joyful life with it. Life is full of hardships. There are many ways to deal with them. I turn to a community who can laugh with me, appreciate with me, cry with me, suffer with me and who fully understands me.

The diabetes community is my second family.

Chapter 19:
The Gila Monster: A Venomous Miracle

GLP-1 stands for Glucagon-Like Peptide-1. GLP-1 is a gut hormone. Before 1992, GLP-1 had no clinical relevance. Why? Because despite a then-ninety-year old paper and many experimental advancements, GLP-1 degraded too quickly to be useful in any clinical trials, tests or enhancements. Until Dr. John Eng stumbled upon the Gila monster lizard *Heloderma suspectum* and the proteins found in its venom.

What does GLP-1 do?

GLP-1 is a hormone found in the small intestine. The small intestine absorbs food from the gastrointestinal tract into the bloodstream. From there the food travels to the liver. The liver processes all of the fats, carbohydrates, proteins and nutrients before dispersing them throughout the body via the bloodstream.

Noted by scientists Bayliss and Starling, GLP-1 specifically activates in the presence of carbohydrates or its building block glucose. GLP-1 causes an *incretin* effect to reduce the amount of glucose circulating the blood stream. The incretin effect stimulates amplified insulin secretions from the pancreas. The incretin effect also inhibits the conversion of stored glycogen in the liver to active blood-circulating glucose.

Insulin helps regulate glucose intake into cells from the bloodstream. Insulin acts like a key, unlocking cell glucose transporters or gates. Inside the cell, glucose takes part in a process called cellular respiration.

Cellular respiration uses glucose, alongside the oxygen we breathe, to form energy molecules called ATP. The body uses ATP in innumerable cellular processes. Without ATP, the body would collapse. Glucose intake into cells also helps maintain clear blood vessels with stable blood glucose concentrations outside the cells.

Blood glucose concentrations must remain in a narrow range. Enough glucose must constantly circulate the blood stream to allow ATP production at all hours of the day, even when not consuming food. However, a surplus glucose concentration will act like plaque and clog the blood stream.

Studies undertaken in 1993 by Michael Nauck of the Department of Medicine at Georg-August-Universität in Germany showed that GLP-1 could account for up to 70% of insulin secretions in response to nutrient uptake.

Further studies by Nauck also showed GLP-1 to induce feelings of satiety and satisfaction. These studies also showed GLP-1 to cause a delay in the movement of food from the stomach into the small intestine, delaying absorption. In this manner, GLP-1 helps induce weight loss, a very beneficial side effect for anyone suffering from obesity.

Thus, GLP-1 is very relevant with respect to the major disease dealing with insulin: diabetes mellitus.

Breaking Down Diabetes:

The American Diabetes Association breaks down diabetes mellitus into two major sub-categories: type 1 and type 2.

Type 1 diabetes mellitus deals with the destruction of the pancreatic islets of Langerhans, the cells responsible for insulin production. The immune system, for some unknown reason, goes rogue and mistakenly identifies these islets of Langerhans as foreign and threatening. The immune system destroys them in an autoimmune attack. Insulin production screeches to a halt.

Type 2 diabetes mellitus, on the other hand, deals with insulin resistance. Here, the body, through a still-unknown mechanism, responds poorly to insulin activity.

The pancreas still initially produces insulin. In fact, in many early stages of type 2 diabetes mellitus as well as prediabetes, the pancreas secretes insulin in excessive quantities to make up for the growing insensitivity.

However, over time, if the pancreas detects no remarkable response to increased insulin, insulin production diminishes to a halt, similar to type 1 diabetes mellitus.

In essence, if insulin is a key to a cell gate for glucose, type 1 diabetes occurs when the key is lost, and type 2 when the gate is broken.

How does GLP-1 interact with Diabetes Mellitus?

GLP-1 can help increase insulin production thereby having a positive effect on pancreatic health and overall survival. This would be especially useful for recently diagnosed type 2 diabetics with a still-functioning pancreas.

Sufficient GLP-1 concentration would allow for increased insulin production and pancreatic cell health. This could potentially stop pancreatic shut down as seen in the late stages of uncontrolled type 2 diabetes.

The problem with GLP-1, however, is that it has a very short half-life. Enzymes degrade GLP-1 very quickly. Its concentration drops by half every 2-5 minutes. In essence, less than 10% of the original concentration remains after 6-15 minutes. Would this cause a problem in nondiabetics who lack insulin resistance? No.

In type 2 diabetics, however, decreased insulin sensitivity means the body needs more insulin for an effect. Without medication, type 2 diabetics will always hover in mild or severe hyperglycaemia—high blood glucose levels. Type 2 diabetics, to counter insulin resistance, need an insulin secretion larger than what the GLP-1 hormone can provide.

Heloderma suspectum

Source: Bluesg9 from Wikimedia Commons

The Gila monster Heloderma suspectum can hold a steady blood sugar for hours after its last meal.

In the 1990s, Dr. John Eng, an endocrinologist at the Veterans Administration Center in the Bronx, USA, studied the Gila monster lizard Heloderma suspectum.

He observed the Gila monster hold a steady blood glucose level for hours after its meal without affecting its health. He analyzed its venom and found a protein called exendin-4.

Exendin-4, he determined, possesses a 53% similarity to the human GLP-1 hormone. He found these similarities in its active receptor regions, allowing a function identical to GLP-1.

The difference, however, lies in the stability of the exendin-4 peptide hormone. Exendin-4 has a half-life of 2.4 hours. This allows exendin-4 to remain active for about 8 hours, in a stark contrast to the measly 15 minutes of activity GLP-1 can hold. Exendin-4 thus allows for a much greater effect than regular GLP-1.

Dr. Eng co-operated with the pharmaceutical company, Amylin Pharmceuticals, to modify exendin-4 into a usable drug. This cooperation culminated in 2005 with the release of the injectable drug Byetta, the first GLP-1 receptor agonist (GLP-1 RA). As an agonist, it helps initiate biological cascades which culminate in GLP-1 hormone release.

GLP-1 Receptor Agonists in 2020

In the 15 intervening years since Amylin Pharmaceuticals released Byetta, more and more GLP-1 analogues like Byetta have surfaced. Each analogue improved upon the core function of GLP-1 RAs.

Recently, in September 2019, the company Novo Nordisk made a major breakthrough in the form of the newly FDA-approved Rybelsus. Rybelsus, unlike all the other GLP-1 RAs before it, requires oral consumption once a day instead of an injection.

Sources:

Ahrén, B. (2003). Gut peptides and type 2 diabetes mellitus treatment. *Current Diabetes Reports*, *3*(5), pp. 365-372, https://doi.org/10.1007/s11892-003-0079-9

Blueag9. (Photographer). Heloderma suspectum [digital image], https://commons.wikimedia.org/wiki/File:Gila_monster2.JPG#filelinks

Diabetes Association, American. (2012). Diagnosis and classification of diabetes mellitus. *Diabetes Care*, *36*(Supplement_1), pp. S67-S74, https://doi.org/10.2337/dc13-s067

Editors, B. (2020). Cellular respiration. *Biology Dictionary*, https://biologydictionary.net/cellular-respiration/

Furman, B. (2012). The development of Byetta (exenatide) from the venom of the Gila monster as an anti-diabetic agent. *Toxicon*, *59*(4), pp. 464-471, https://doi.org/10.1016/j.toxicon.2010.12.016

Holst, J., Knop, F., Vilsboll, T., Krarup, T., & Madsbad, S. (2011). Loss of Incretin effect is a specific, important, and early characteristic of type 2 diabetes. *Diabetes Care*, *34*(Supplement_2), pp. S251-S257, https://doi.org/10.2337/dc11-s227

Hui, H., Farilla, L., Merkel, P., & Perfetti, R. (2002). The short half-life of glucagon-like peptide-1 in plasma does not reflect its long-lasting beneficial effects. *European Journal Of Endocrinology*, pp. 863-869, https://doi.org/10.1530/eje.0.1460863

Knudsen, L., & Lau, J. (2019). The discovery and development of Liraglutide and Semaglutide. *Frontiers In Endocrinology*, *10*, https://doi.org/10.3389/fendo.2019.00155

Nauck, M., Heimesaat, M., Orskov, C., Holst, J., Ebert, R., & Creutzfeldt, W. (1993). Preserved incretin activity of glucagon-like peptide 1 [7-36 amide] but not of synthetic human gastric inhibitory polypeptide in patients with type-2 diabetes mellitus. *Journal Of Clinical Investigation*, *91*(1), pp. 301-307, https://doi.org/10.1172/jci116186

Nauck, M., Niedereichholz, U., Ettler, R., Holst, J., Ørskov, C., Ritzel, R., & Schmiegel, W. (1997). Glucagon-like peptide 1 inhibition of gastric emptying outweighs its insulinotropic effects in healthy humans. *American Journal Of Physiology-Endocrinology And Metabolism*, *273*(5), E981-E988, https://doi.org/10.1152/ajpendo.1997.273.5.e981

Parkes, D., Jodka, C., Smith, P., Nayak, S., Rinehart, L., & Gingerich, R. et al. (2001). Pharmacokinetic actions of exendin-4 in the rat: Comparison with glucagon-like peptide-1. *Drug Development Research*, *53*(4), pp. 260-267, https://doi.org/10.1002/ddr.1195

Singh, G., Eng, J., & Raufman, J. (1994). Use of 125I-[Y39]exendin-4 to characterize exendin receptors on dispersed pancreatic acini and gastric chief cells from guinea pig. *Regulatory Peptides*, *53*(1), pp. 47-59, https://doi.org/10.1016/0167-0115(94)90158-9

Sonia, T., & Sharma, C. (2014). Diabetes mellitus – an overview. *Oral Delivery Of Insulin*, pp. 1-57, https://doi.org/10.1533/9781908818683.1

Wright, E. E., Jr, & Aroda, V. R. (2020). Clinical review of the efficacy and safety of oral semaglutide in patients with type 2 diabetes considered for injectable GLP-1 receptor agonist therapy or currently on insulin therapy. *Postgraduate medicine*, pp. 1–11. Advance online publication, https://doi.org/10.1080/00325481.2020.1798127

Yuan, W., Cai, Y., Liangming Wei, L., Ma, L., Huang, X., Tao, A., & Liu, Z. (2013). Long-acting preparations of exenatide. *Drug Design, Development And Therapy*, 963, https://doi.org/10.2147/dddt.s46970

Zaccardi, F., Webb, D., Yates, T., & Davies, M. (2015). Pathophysiology of type 1 and type 2 diabetes mellitus: A 90-year perspective. *Postgraduate Medical Journal*, *92*(1084), pp. 63-69, https://doi.org/10.1136/postgradmedj-2015-133281

Chapter 20:
GLP-1 RAs: From Injectable to SNACable

Fifteen years ago, Amelyin Pharmaceuticals cooperated with Dr. John Eng to create the drug Byetta, a compound based off of a protein called exendin-4. Dr. Eng isolated exendin-4 from the venom of the Gila monster Heloderma suspectum.

Scientists classify exendin-4 as a receptor agonist (RA) of the human GLP-1 hormone. As an agonist, it helps initiate GLP-1 release. While found in lizard venom, exendin-4 can accomplish the same function as the human GLP-1 hormone, hence the term receptor agonist.

What Does GLP-1 Do?

GLP-1 is a peptide hormone found in the small intestine. The GLP-1 protein functions only in the presence of the glucose or carbohydrates that we consume in our meals. The activated GLP-1 protein then travels from the small intestine to the pancreas, wherein it commands the pancreas to secrete the hormone insulin.

Insulin acts like a key. It unlocks the glucose "cell gates" and allows glucose molecules circulating the bloodstream to enter cells. Inside a cell, glucose participates in a process called cellular respiration. Cellular respiration uses glucose alongside the oxygen we breathe to form usable energy molecules called ATP. Without ATP, our bodies would collapse.

In a healthy human body, the pancreas secretes insulin and the body readily accepts it without a problem. However, in a diabetic body, there exists a noticeable problem regarding insulin—a diabetic pancreas cannot produce insulin anymore. The American Diabetes Association classifies this as type 1 diabetes mellitus.

The American Diabetes Association also classifies a second type 2 diabetes mellitus. Here, the glucose cell gates throughout the body break down. While the pancreas may still produce insulin, the cells cannot interact with insulin as easily as before. They grow insulin resistant. The body then requires more insulin to deal with a smaller load of glucose.

In 1993, Michael Nauck at Georg-August-Universität in Germany showed that the GLP-1 hormone response could account for up to 70% of insulin secretions in response to nutrient uptake.

However, GLP-1 is very unstable. It has a minuscule half-life of 2-5 minutes. Hence any time a load of glucose activates a wave of GLP-1 hormones, this wave will diminish to practically zero in less than 30 minutes. For type 2 diabetics in need of longer and larger insulin secretions, the native human GLP-1 hormone isn't enough.

By comparison, exendin-4 has a relatively longer half-life of 2.4 hours and remains active for about 8 hours.

In the fifteen years since Byetta came onto the market, scientists have improved GLP-1 RAs significantly, both in their half-life and their activity period. In those fifteen years, however, until recently, patients could only take GLP-1 RAs via injection. An oral tablet did not exist.

In November 2018, Dr. Stephen Buckley at the company Novo Nordisk helped formulate and develop an oral tablet.

Why Was Oral Delivery Impossible before?

The chemical nature of the GLP-1 peptide hormone and its analogues previously made oral delivery impossible. GLP-1 is a peptide hormone found in the small intestine. A peptide is a biological molecule made of amino acids. Amino acids are the building blocks of proteins. The difference between a peptide and a protein simply lies in the size. Peptides are considerably smaller than full-fledged proteins.

Regardless of size, however, amino acid-based structures cannot survive intact in the stomach.

The stomach contains a very acidic environment, with a pH range of 2-4. For reference, such an environment ranges anywhere from 1,000 to 100,000 times more acidic than neutral water. The acid itself isn't the direct problem. The high acidity serves as an ideal environment for the peptide-cleaving enzyme pepsin to function. Pepsin cleaves peptides and proteins into small segments. This allows for easy protein digestion. Thus, under regular circumstances, patients cannot orally consume any peptide hormone or medication.

Why is Oral Delivery of GLP-1 RAs possible now?

Stephen Buckley and his team at Novo Nordisk experimented with one of the latest GLP-1 RAs: *semaglutide*. They paired it with a molecule called *sodium N-[8-(2-hydroxybenzoyl) amino] caprylate*, also known as *SNAC*. SNAC is an absorption enhancer. It helps allow different drugs easier access to the bloodstream via a variety of mechanisms. Buckley and his team aimed to determine these mechanisms through a variety of experiments.

Co-formulation Versus Co-administration

Buckley co-formulated SNAC with semaglutide. Co-formulation differs from co-administration where patients take multiple separate drugs at once. A co-formulation involves both semaglutide and SNAC bound to each other in a single tablet. This allows both molecules to stay extremely close together for as long as possible. Such an association is important given the unique absorption enhancement that SNAC allows.

A SNAC In The Stomach

Buckley and his team first determined the absorption location and time of the new drug, using *scintigraphic* imaging. A scintigraphic image uses gamma radiation to highlight the absorbed drug within the gastrointestinal tract. Unlike an X-ray, however, scientists detect radioactive elements attached to the drug and form an image based on this radioactivity. Where the radioactive element eventually disperses in the digestive tract is the drug absorption site.

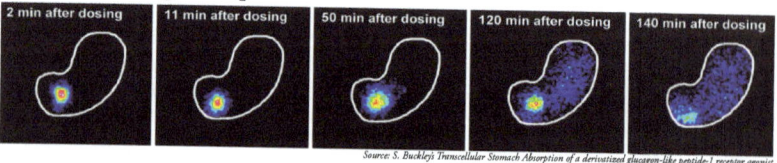

Source: S. Buckley's *Transcellular Stomach Absorption of a derivatized glucagon-like peptide-1 receptor agonist*

A gamma scintigraphic image showing the eventual complete erosion of an oral semaglutide/SNAC tablet over the course of 140 minutes. The radioactive isotopes remain concentrated around the initial tablet deposit site.

In Buckley's case, scintigraphic imaging showed the stomach as the absorption site instead of the small intestine. The imaging showed the tablet core slowly dissolving, with no visible radioactive core remaining after 140 minutes.

Measurements showed the stomach area directly underneath the tablet core deposit containing semaglutide and SNAC concentrations over 10 times higher than in areas six centimetres away from the core.

This localization highlights the need for the co-formulation used. Both SNAC and semaglutide do not disperse too far away from wherever in the stomach the tablet ends up.

Co-administration of two separate tablets could lead to two separate regions in the stomach. One region would have a high SNAC concentration and the other a high semaglutide concentration. There may perhaps only be a small overlap in the two regions. Co-administration would thus be far less effective than co-formulation.

The Miracle That Is SNAC

Under regular circumstances, proteins and peptides cannot pass through the stomach unscathed. The acidic environment allows for the peptide-cleaving pepsin enzyme to thrive.

With the inclusion of SNAC in the co-formulation, however, SNAC serves as a pH buffer. SNAC transiently neutralizes the stomach pH, making it more akin to water than acid and rendering pepsin inactive.

This allows semaglutide to survive for a time until the stomach walls absorb it. Usually the stomach wall would not absorb molecules like semaglutide due to their large size.

However, being co-formulated, SNAC makes the stomach wall more permeable for the semaglutide to pass through and bind to the neighbouring GLP-1 receptors.

The Present: Rybelsus

Buckley's research was crucial in the development of Novo Nordisk's newest drug: the world's first oral GLP-1 RA Rybelsus. The USA FDA (Food and Drug Administration) approved the drug in September 2019.

The Future:

SNAC successfully worked as an absorption enhancer for semaglutide and GLP-1 RAs. However, this is only the beginning for the oral delivery of peptide hormones and medication.

As Buckley pointed out in his research, SNAC, as well as other enhancers, do not follow a one-size-fits-all solution model. Different peptides need very specific absorption enhancers. This is why, Buckley suggests, that such endeavours might not have advanced as fast as one might expect.

Sources:

Brayden, D., Hill, T., Fairlie, D., Maher, S., & Mrsny, R. (2020). Systemic delivery of peptides by the oral route: Formulation and medicinal chemistry approaches. *Advanced Drug Delivery Reviews*, https://doi.org/10.1016/j.addr.2020.05.007

Buckley, S., Bækdal, T., Vegge, A., Maarbjerg, S., Pyke, C., & Ahnfelt-Rønne, J. et al. (2018). Transcellular stomach absorption of a derivatized glucagon-like peptide-1 receptor agonist. *Science Translational Medicine, 10*(467), https://doi.org/10.1126/scitranslmed.aar7047

Diabetes Association, American. (2012). Diagnosis and classification of diabetes mellitus. *Diabetes Care, 36*(Supplement_1), pp. S67-S74, https://doi.org/10.2337/dc13-s067

Editors, B. (2020). Cellular respiration. *Biology Dictionary*, https://biologydictionary.net/cellular-respiration/

Hui, H., Farilla, L., Merkel, P., & Perfetti, R. (2002). The short half-life of glucagon-like peptide-1 in plasma does not reflect its long-lasting beneficial effects. *European Journal Of Endocrinology*, pp. 863-869, https://doi.org/10.1530/eje.0.1460863

Knudsen, L., & Lau, J. (2019). The discovery and development of Liraglutide and Semaglutide. *Frontiers In Endocrinology*, *10*, https://doi.org/10.3389/fendo.2019.00155

Nauck, M., Heimesaat, M., Orskov, C., Holst, J., Ebert, R., & Creutzfeldt, W. (1993). Preserved incretin activity of glucagon-like peptide 1 [7-36 amide] but not of synthetic human gastric inhibitory polypeptide in patients with type-2 diabetes mellitus. *Journal Of Clinical Investigation*, *91*(1), pp. 301-307, https://doi.org/10.1172/jci116186

Pepsin. (2021). *Oxford English Dictionary Online*, https://www.oxfordreference.com/view/10.1093/oi/authority.20110803100316151

Scintigraphy. (2021). *Oxford English Dictionary Online*, https://www.oxfordreference.com/view/10.1093/oi/authority.20110803100447831

Singh, G., Eng, J., & Raufman, J. (1994). Use of 125I-[Y39]exendin-4 to characterize exendin receptors on dispersed pancreatic acini and gastric chief cells from guinea pig. *Regulatory Peptides*, *53*(1), pp. 47-59, https://doi.org/10.1016/0167-0115(94)90158-9

Wright, E. E., Jr, & Aroda, V. R. (2020). Clinical review of the efficacy and safety of oral semaglutide in patients with type 2 diabetes considered for injectable GLP-1 receptor agonist therapy or currently on insulin therapy. *Postgraduate Medicine*, pp. 1–11, https://doi.org/10.1080/00325481.2020.1798127

Chapter 21
Inverse Vaccines: Immune System Re-Education

Scientists call the physiological regulation of sugar or glucose molecules in the body glucose homeostasis. Glucose refers not only to simple white sugar, but exists in most foods as carbohydrates. The body breaks down carbohydrates into glucose during digestion. These glucose molecules take part in a process called cellular respiration to form energy molecules called ATP. Countless physiological processes require ATP to occur.

Glucose molecules travel through the bloodstream before entering blood vessel-adjacent cells where cellular respiration takes place. However, due to their relatively large molecular size, glucose molecules enter through specific glucose transporters, akin to cell gates. These gates require a key to grant entrance: the hormone insulin.

The pancreas produces insulin and maintains glucose homeostasis.

When Glucose Homeostasis Goes Out Of Whack

In diabetes mellitus, glucose homeostasis flees out of control. According to the American Diabetes Association, this loss of control usually occurs in one of two different ways:

The pancreas cannot produce insulin anymore; the key is lost. Scientists call this type 1 diabetes mellitus.

The cells cannot react to insulin as well as before; the cell gates rust shut. Scientists call this type 2 diabetes mellitus.

For type 1 diabetes mellitus specifically, no insulin means no cellular access to glucose. No access means a deprivation of energy inside the cells. No access means a plaque-like accumulation of glucose in the blood vessels outside the cells. Both factors, compounded, lead to a slow, but painfully inevitable, fatality if not treated.

Before 1922, diabetes mellitus was a death sentence; no effective treatment existed.

Since 1922, however, scientists beginning with Dr. Fredrick Banting of Canada found methods to extract insulin from animals. By the tail end of the twentieth century, insulin synthesis in laboratories was possible. These discoveries allowed diabetics opportunities to live full lives.

While a miracle, the discovery of insulin still remains a treatment to diabetes mellitus, not a cure. A cure would render manual insulin management a figment of the past.

To date, a cure remains elusive.

The Immune System: Confusion Galore

Over the last four decades, type 1 diabetes mellitus treatment shifted from simply injecting insulin to methods surrounding the still-incomplete disease pathology and origin involving the immune system.

According to the National Institute of Allergy and Infectious Diseases, the immune system functions via a group of different white blood cells. Some of these white blood cells, called dendritic cells, serve as the sentinels of the immune system. Dendritic cells, named for their probing or tree-like shape, search for foreign objects like viruses, with specific recognition markers called *antigens*.

Inverse Vaccines: Immune System Re-Education

Upon antigen detection, dendritic cells help initiate immune responses and destroy the foreign antigen-presenting threat. Immune responses use certain chemicals, hormones and enzymes which manifest to the human eye as inflammations.

Type 1 diabetes usually occurs due to an autoimmune reaction, where the immune system goes haywire. For some currently unknown reason, the immune system mistakenly identifies the insulin-producing beta cells in the pancreas as threatening and destroys them.

However, this destruction does not necessarily happen overnight. As a consequence, a person may be diabetic but not show any symptoms or complications until enough beta cells are destroyed. Even after a diagnosis, some beta cells may still remain, with the autoimmune attack gradually destroying them over time.

Radical Approach: Re-Education, Not Suppression

Many diabetic treatment methods involving the immune system use immunosuppressants to slow down beta cell destruction. However, immunosuppressants cripple the immune system. Hence such strategies haven't succeeded. In the past year, however, Dr. Bart Roep and his team at the Leiden University Medical Center focused their research on "[educating] the immune system to teach it what *not* to do," instead of immune system suppression.

The idea works akin to a vaccine. Scientists use vaccines to aid the immune system in destroying viruses. The immune system can usually fight off weak viruses, like the common cold. However, the immune system functions on a slow first response. It possesses no prior experience against novel viruses and takes time constructing a correct countermeasure. With new, severe viruses, such a response may not be fast enough.

According to the National Institute of Allergy and Infectious Diseases, vaccines aid the immune system to overcome this inexperience. The relationship between vaccines and viruses can be likened to exam papers. A person does not know what questions will appear on an upcoming exam. However, if they can access past exam papers, they can get an idea on what to expect and prepare accordingly.

Similarly, vaccines present a harmless, inert virus to the immune system, similar to the harmful, active threat. The immune system ingests the vaccine virus and forms a protocol for any future threats—a memory. This allows for a fast, efficient response.

Dr. Roep developed what he calls an "inverse" vaccine. Because the diabetic immune system attacks the pancreatic beta cells, an inverse vaccine would theoretically erase this twisted memory.

"It is a radical approach that does not involve immune suppression," states Dr. Roep. "[Rather], it engages the immune system and causes desensitization [to the beta cells], like allergy treatments." The immune system would no longer see healthy beta cells as enemies it needs to attack.

How to form an inverse vaccine:

Dr. Roep developed an inverse vaccine by cultivating special *tolerogenic dendritic cells (tolDCs)*. Tolerogenic dendritic cells play a special role in mediating immune response and tolerance.

Immune tolerance refers to an immune system's unresponsiveness to certain compounds, molecule and substances. The immune system effectively tolerates and co-exists with these compounds. Many tolerances innately exist to stop the immune system from attacking antigen-presenting cells native to the body. An autoimmune attack effectively inverts certain tolerances, making them appear foreign.

Dr. Roep thus took white blood cells destined to become future tolDCs from diabetic patients and modified them to tolerate pancreatic islet cells. He accomplished this by submerging the cells in a bath with a high vitamin D3 concentration.

Vitamin D3 regulates immune system function by reducing inflammatory responses. These vitamin-bathed tolDCs consequently became anti-inflammatory. Before introducing them back into the body, Dr. Roep treated them with a fragment of proinsulin.

Proinsulin is the inactive form of insulin, a form produced by pancreatic cells and eventually processed into regular insulin before travelling through the bloodstream towards target cells.

By introducing these modified tolDCs into a patient, Dr. Roep hopes to halt beta cell destruction in diabetics. This could possibly give an effective cure to those with enough functioning beta cells.

Currently, Dr. Roep and his team successfully completed a small phase 1a trial on 9 long-term type 1 diabetics, each diagnosed for over an average 12 years. Because of the very human nature of proinsulin and the tolDCs, the team could not use larger animal trials.

The trial helped show an initial margin of safety. Each of the patients suffered no adverse vaccine-related side effects. However, given the length of time since diagnosis, none of the patients possessed an adequate number of insulin-producing beta cells to determine any positive vaccine benefits beyond safety.

Dr. Roep and his team next hope to conduct a phase 1b trial on more recently diagnosed individuals, in hopes of ascertaining a more complete safety profile as well as any more noticeable benefits. If this study succeeds, the team can move on to a larger phase 2 study and beyond.

Sources:

Burke, C. (2020). Developing an 'inverse vaccine' for type 1 diabetes | BioSpace. BioSpace, https://www.biospace.com/article/developing-an-inverse-vaccine-for-type-1-diabetes/.

British Society for Immunology. (2020). Dendritic cells|British society for immunology. Immunology.org, https://www.immunology.org/public-information/bitesized-immunology/cells/dendritic-cells.

Diabetes Association, American. (2012). Diagnosis and classification of diabetes mellitus. *Diabetes Care, 36*(Supplement_1), pp. S67-S74, https://doi.org/10.2337/dc13-s067

Editors, B. (2020). Cellular respiration. *Biology Dictionary*, https://biologydictionary.net/cellular-respiration/

Jansen, M., Spiering, R., Ludwig, I. S., van Eden, W., Hilkens, C., & Broere, F. (2019). Matured tolerogenic dendritic cells effectively inhibit autoantigen specific CD4+ T cells in a murine arthritis model. *Frontiers in Immunology, 10*, 2068, https://doi.org/10.3389/fimmu.2019.02068

National Institute of Allergy and Infectious Diseases. (2020). Features of an Immune Response. Niaid.nih.gov, https://www.niaid.nih.gov/research/immune-response-features.

National Institute of Allergy and Infectious Diseases. (2020). Immune tolerance. Niaid.nih.gov, https://www.niaid.nih.gov/research/immune-tolerance.

Nicholas, D., Odumosu, O., & Langridge, W. H. (2011). Autoantigen based vaccines for type 1 diabetes. *Discovery Medicine, 11*(59), pp. 293–301.

Nikolic, T., Zwaginga, J., Uitbeijerse, B., Woittiez, N., de Koning, E., Aanstoot, H., & Roep, B. (2020). Safety and feasibility of intradermal injection with tolerogenic dendritic cells pulsed with proinsulin peptide—for type 1 diabetes. *The Lancet Diabetes & Endocrinology, 8*(6), pp. 470-472, https://doi.org/10.1016/s2213-8587(20)30104-2

Yin, K., & Agrawal, D. K. (2014). Vitamin D and inflammatory diseases. *Journal of Inflammation Research, 7*, pp. 69–87, https://doi.org/10.2147/JIR.S63898

Zaccardi, F., Webb, D., Yates, T., & Davies, M. (2015). Pathophysiology of type 1 and type 2 diabetes mellitus: A 90-year perspective. *Postgraduate Medical Journal, 92*(1084), pp. 63-69, https://doi.org/10.1136/postgradmedj-2015-133281

Chapter 22

Aceruloplasminemia and Diabetes Mellitus

The *New England Journal of Medicine* reported a rare disease case this past November. In Boston, Massachusetts, a neighbour saw a 59-year-old woman, let's call her Mrs. K, in her car one winter evening. The next day, the neighbour found her in the exact same position, unresponsive. The neighbour could not wake up Mrs. K.

Upon hospital admission, Mrs. K remained unconscious. She could not provide a medical history but responded to tactile stimuli. Doctor David Caplan, a neurologist, sought to understand how she reached her current situation by expunging additional information from her medical records.

As stated in her medical records, "[Mrs. K] did not smoke tobacco, drink alcohol, or use illicit substances." However, a slew of different diseases litter her file, such as asthma and leukaemia. Most notably however, she suffers from *diabetes mellitus, diabetic retinopathy* and *chronic anemia.*

Diabetes Mellitus

According to the American Diabetes Association, diabetes mellitus occurs when the body cannot properly utilize the carbohydrates we consume.

After the small intestine absorbs carbohydrates, the body breaks them down into smaller sugar or glucose molecules. These glucose molecules circulate the bloodstream. They are necessary for a process called cellular respiration.

Cellular respiration manipulates glucose to form a usable energy molecule called ATP. ATP powers physiological processes all over the body. Without ATP and by proxy cellular respiration, the body would collapse and die. Cellular respiration happens inside cells lining the bloodstream. Hence, glucose molecules must exit the bloodstream and enter cells for cellular respiration to occur.

However, due to their relatively large molecular size, glucose molecules can only enter cells through specific glucose transporters, akin to cell gates. These gates require a key to function: the hormone insulin. The pancreas produces insulin and manages glucose regulation or homeostasis.

If glucose cannot enter cells, it causes a deficiency in energy and ATP production inside the cell. It also causes a build-up of glucose in the bloodstream outside the cell, like an aggressive plaque. Scientists refer to this condition as hyperglycaemia.

With diabetes mellitus type 1, the pancreas cannot produce insulin. The key is lost.

Type 1 diabetics inject insulin into their bodies to compensate for the crippled pancreas. Because the pancreas, which used to manage glucose homeostasis autonomously, is defunct, diabetics must manually keep their blood glucose levels in check.

Type 1 diabetics used to inject insulin using needles. Now, due to advancing technology, many use insulin pumps in place of injections. Pumps continuously deliver insulin throughout the day through a subcutaneous patch, like a poor pancreatic caricature.

While the pump does continuously injects insulin to keep blood sugar levels at a constant level, diabetics must manually calculate how many carbohydrates they will consume in a meal and input a proportionate load of insulin.

Mrs. K uses an insulin pump. She also developed diabetic retinopathy, a progressive diabetic complication which deteriorates eyesight and can cause blindness.

Chronic Anemia

Chronic anemia defines people with a continuously low number of red blood cells. Red blood cells play a crucial role in transporting oxygen from the lungs to the rest of the body. They act like large cruise ships, full of important passenger proteins called hemoglobin.

These hemoglobin proteins contain iron molecules. The iron molecules give the blood its red colour. The iron molecules bind oxygen molecules and transport them to various cells for use. The more hemoglobin a person has, the more oxygen they can transport in a given time.

Mrs. K not only possessed a low red blood cell count, but her red blood cells were smaller than usual. They contained less hemoglobin per cell. Scientists call this specific variant of the disease *microcytic anemia*. Due to microcytic anemia, Mrs. K has both a reduced oxygen carrying capacity and a low amount of free iron circulating the blood.

The Background Check

The most intriguing information about Mrs. K came when Dr. Caplan conducted a background check asking her neighbours, family and endocrinologist about her health. He found that while for most of her life she "managed her diabetes with a high degree of sophistication," her mental health noticeably declined in the last two years.

She grew paranoid and thought that someone hacked her computer to spy on her. Her endocrinologist, using a Mini-Mental State Examination to test her cognitive function, found a deficit in "short term object recall, attention, and calculation."

More recently, two weeks before the incident, family members found handwritten holiday cards with illegible handwriting where once it was immaculate.

These cognitive defects translated into her diabetes management. Blood glucose tests revealed a glucose concentration level of 17.8 millimoles per litre. Blood glucose concentrations should usually remain around 3.9 to 5.6 millimoles per litre. Mrs. K had too much glucose in her blood; she was very hyperglycaemic. She did not take a proper amount of insulin.

Her reduced cognitive function led Dr. Caplan to consider multiple diseases and conditions which could adversely impact her brain and nervous system. He consulted MRI scans to find any physical abnormalities in the brain.

The MRIs showed lesion injury patterns in the brain consistent with iron mineralization. Similar to plaque and glucose build-up in bloodstreams, brain mineralization can immensely impede certain brain and nervous system functions.

The questions then arose: How does an iron-deficient person build up an iron accumulation and why does this accumulation occur?

As Dr. Caplan reviewed the scientific literature, he identified "10 [possible] forms of neurodegeneration with brain iron accumulation, [with each disorder] associated with a specific genetic mutation. Most of these diseases first develop in childhood or adolescence, but a few develop in adulthood."

Aceruloplasminemia and Diabetes Mellitus

Genetic disorders cause mutations in certain genes, mutating whatever biological pathway and end result may usually occur. Certain disorders hinder the proper integration of iron in our bodies.

Iron Overload

The one disease that stood out to Dr. Caplan was the rare disease aceruloplasminemia [A-seru-low-plasmi-nemia]. Aceruloplasminemia occurs most frequently in Japan at a mere 1 in 2,000,000 marriages. Hence, the disease remains under-researched. Aceruloplasminemia occurs when a DNA mutation causes the lack of expression of the protein ceruloplasmin.

Ceruloplasmin is a ferroxidase enzyme. An enzyme functions as a catalyst, helping facilitate certain biochemical transformations and chemical pathways. As a ferroxidase enzyme, ceruloplasmin helps convert ferrous (Fe^{2+}) iron into ferric (Fe^{3+}) iron.

Ferrous iron is soluble in blood and relatively stable. It integrates with red blood cells and helps carry oxygen. However, excessive ferrous iron will form iron deposits in tissues. While iron is necessary for certain physiological functions like blood cell formation, excessive iron can cause cell death.

Ferric iron, on the other hand, is insoluble in blood and relatively unstable. However, it usually stays bound to storage molecules like the protein ferritin. Ferritin helps keep a reserve of iron which can be used should the need arise.

In Mrs. K's case, Dr. Caplan took a blood test checking for ceruloplasmin levels. If she had aceruloplasminemia, ceruloplasmin levels would be undetectable.

Ceruloplasmin levels were undetectable.

A further genetic test confirmed the diagnosis.

Confusingly enough, however, Mrs. K had very elevated ferritin levels, a marker of high blood iron levels. In reality, due to aceruloplasminemia, Mrs. K could not transform ferrous iron into ferric iron.

The excessive ferrous iron could not integrate into many red blood cells due to Mrs. K's microcytic anemia. Hence, the ferrous iron formed iron deposits in several organs, including the brain, the retina and the pancreas.

Because excessive iron can cause cell death, the iron depositions resulted in the two-year cognitive degeneration, the increasing blindness and the diabetes mellitus. The body, unaware of its inability to transform ferrous iron into ferric iron, kept increasing ferritin levels in hopes of reducing the iron deposits and safely storing them for future use.

To help treat Mrs. K, Dr. Caplan initiated iron chelation therapy. Iron chelation therapy forces iron excretion and thereby eliminates iron overload. To accommodate for Mrs. K's paradoxical microcytic anemia, Dr. Caplan injected her with ceruloplasmin-rich plasma. While she cannot produce ceruloplasmin on her own, the injection allowed a rescue of Mrs. K's demented iron homeostasis.

The treatment saved Mrs. K but it took two months of in-hospital care before the hospital could release her. She still suffers from moderate cognitive impairment to the present day. Mrs. K now lives in a longterm memory-care facility close to family.

Sources:

Caplan, D., Rapalino, O., Karaa, A., Rosovsky, R., & Uljon, S. (2020). Case 35-2020: A 59-year-old woman with ype 1 diabetes mellitus and obtundation. *New England Journal Of Medicine*, 383(20), pp. 1974-1983, https://doi.org/10.1056/nejmcpc2002412

Diabetes Association, American. (2012). Diagnosis and classification of diabetes mellitus. *Diabetes Care*, 36(Supplement_1), pp. S67-S74, https://doi.org/10.2337/dc13-s067

Editors, B. (2020). Cellular respiration. *Biology Dictionary*, https://biologydictionary.net/cellular-respiration/

Granick, S. (1946). Ferritin: Its properties and significance for iron metabolism. *Chemical Reviews*, 38(3), pp. 379-403, https://doi.org/10.1021/cr60121a001

Learning, L. (2020). Transport of gases in human bodily fluids|Boundless biology. *Courses.lumenlearning.com*, https://courses.lumenlearning.com/boundless-biology/chapter/transport-of-gases-in-human-bodily-fluids/

Roberti, M., Borges Filho, H. M., Gonçalves, C. H., & Lima, F. L. (2011). Aceruloplasminemia: A rare disease - diagnosis and treatment of two cases. *Revista brasileira de hematologia e hemoterapia*, 33(5), pp. 389–392, https://doi.org/10.5581/1516-8484.20110104

Chapter 23

Outsider Once Again

August 8, 2018

The command echoes in my head as I make my way through the overcrowded Camp Huronda cafeteria: "Abdullah, you will shadow the Beavers for the day, headed by Jamie, Alex and Kyle."

Underneath the hot August sun, the camp has already endured three weeks of blazing summer heat. The cafeteria will also probably feel like an oven and reek of sweat, lake water, alcohol swabs and glucose tablets.

About one hundred and twenty campers, counsellors and medical staff squeeze around blue, red, green and yellow tables. Cabins are separated by age and gender.

I struggle past campers, bustling counsellors and a wild singalong to Frozen's "Let It Go" and finally reach the Beavers' table—eight boys about eight to ten years old. They devour cream of mushroom soup and crackers alongside a fat meat patty burger. Kyle, one of the counsellors, sits on the edge of a bench.

"Hey, Beaver cabin, my name is Abdullah and I'll be with you folks for the day!" I announce. I hope they heard me. I think they did. Kyle nods. That's a good sign.

Abdullah Sher

I squish myself between two campers and seat myself at the table.

Alright Abdullah, time to interact with campers and be counsellor-like as possible!

The campers chat loudly among themselves. Their conversations overlap with one another, filled with camp memories I only experienced a year ago, camp memories I was not a part of this year. Their conversations blend in with the entire cafeteria into one unintelligible sea of white noise. I stay silent. I don't know which conversation to inject myself into.

What would I even say if I intruded upon one?

It's déjà vu. Last August, I attended Camp Huronda as an LDP (Leadership Development Participant). I had to shadow a cabin as an LDP. Coincidentally, it was Kyle's cabin. I kinda sucked. I took the word shadowing too literally. I observed from the sidelines and didn't participate. My LDP counsellor, Benji, cornered me after a day and asked me if I knew any of the campers' names. He told me to write down the names of all of my campers on the spot. I managed to do it but had I shadowed correctly my competence would never have been questioned in the first place.

Now here I am "shadowing" once again.

Outsider, once again.

I hate being the outsider.

"Abdullah, you're shadowing our cabin for the day?" a voice somehow manages to reach me over the roaring "The past is in the past!" line of "Let it Go." I recognize the chill Toronto accent immediately—Jamie, an LDP cabin mate from last year. It's surprising how many similarities we share. Jamie's also from Toronto and I'm from Mississauga, and because he's from the GTA, he's a bit more knowledgeable about South Asian communities than everyone else at camp.

It might not seem too relevant but considering I'm one of only half a dozen brown people at camp, it helps a lot. Most of all, it's just good to see a familiar face.

"I'll be with you folks for your ZAP free time, your afternoon activities, your evening program and finally your night snack. I'll be heading out for Discovery tomorrow morning," I say.

"Ah, sick! One of our co-counsellors, Alex, is on his day off, but other than that, Kyle and I should be here to answer any questions you may have, alright my dude?" Jamie says.

"Alight, thanks a lot man!"

God, I hope I don't mess anything up this time.

August 9, 2018

"You're leaving right now?" Vic asks. Her face scrunches up as her ever-present smile slips for a moment.

"Yeah!" I say loudly over the cafeteria noise blasting at an all-time high. A bittersweet energy lingers in the background. Tomorrow the cafeteria will house a deafening silence. Campers will trudge their way back home in the morning. There will be last-minute high-fives, group hugs and goodbyes, and a ten-minute chorus of continuous tears when campers ride home on the bus.

The next batch of campers arrives on Sunday. Before the silence and goodbyes, however, a final banquet will be held later.

"I wish I could stay for the banquet but the ride to Disco is, like, five hours and that's without any stops along the way," I say.

A banquet dinner is held on the last Thursday of each camp session with one-hour makeup sessions and fancy dresses for the girls who came prepared for a full-on formal and ten-minute showers and dress-shirts for the few boys who decide to not be completely upstaged by the girls.

Or, if you were like me last year, you came to Banquet decked out in a dark blue cape and top hat costume like you were a time-travelling gentleman from the eighteen hundreds because in no other scenario can a guy unironiclly wear a top hat and a cape to dinner.

Banners and streamers flood the cafeteria and curtain the entrance, and tables are lined with colourful tablecloths. Multiple photoshoots precede the banquet on the woodchip-ridden lawn.

The banquet closes with a cheerful yet melancholic exit filled with a simple repeating of "Walking, I'm just walking along, as I'm singing this walking song, I'm just walking along, uh-uh, oh yeah!" as all the campers walk out after dinner for a final time. And I'm gonna miss it all because we have to leave for Discovery. Damn it!

Vic stays silent for a split second. "Well, good luck at Disco!" She puts her smile back on. Her frown lingers in her eyes. Then her hand sticks up. "Can I give you a high-five?"

I answer with a high-five. A high-five and a soft smile.

It might sound like a strange question to an outsider. Why are you asking to give a high-five? Why not ask for a hug? Why not just give a spontaneous hug right away instead?

It's a special high-five because she knows I do not hug girls. I am not comfortable with it, not out of disdain, but out of my religion and respect. And so our high-five is a hug goodbye.

Vic surprises me further.

"Deer Cabin!" she manages to yell over the noisy hall. "Say goodbye to Abdullah!"

"Bye, Abdullah!" the campers chorus.

It takes a few seconds for my mind to register the surprise, and then I break into a grin and wave back.

Vic was one of the August LDPs last year. In our group, there were nine in total, five girls and four guys. I was the newcomer, and Vic, the veteran. I was the oldest and Vic the youngest by two years.

In the beginning, I was awkward and inexperienced, a tall, lumbering nonswimmer who almost drowned on the first day. Yet somehow over the course of the month-long session, our group formed a family-esque dynamic.

I was referred to as the "dad" of the group and Vic the "mom," but without the romance. We were mom and dad because of how we acted to the rest of the cabin. The friendship between us is as deep as the Marianas Trench in the Pacific Ocean.

In the four weeks we were LDPs, Vic was one of the most considerate. She was the most interested when it came to learning about Islam, and who I prayed to and what I said during that prayer. She respected my boundaries and congratulated me with the rest of the cabin when I treaded water for two whole minutes.

As I walk away from the Deer cabin, I look at the burn bracelet on my wrist—the one all LDPs received at the end of their camp session, a memento of that one summer, forever ingrained and forever cherished.

A rumour among the Camp Discovery staff claims two counsellors from Huronda will arrive to assist us because we're short-staffed.

I hope Vic is one of them.

Chapter 24
Runaway Boy

The campsite rented from Camp Woodeden looks the same since the first time I saw it as a camper some five years ago. Camp Woodeden usually runs for most of the summer and is specifically designed for children with physical disabilities to enjoy.

It's why the deep end of the pool (not lake) is a metre-and-a-half deep and why a clear-cut walkway extends throughout camp and why the ground remains flat and woodchip-free. That's also why each cabin is huge and comes equipped with an individual washroom and shower.

Camp Woodeden rented the facility to Diabetes Canada for the week or two that it ran Camp Discovery—the first camp that I attended. I was about to start high school. I was the youngest member of the oldest Maple cabin.

However, when I arrive as a camp counsellor, it takes until cabin assignment night on Saturday to realize the Maple cabin no longer exists. That night we gather outside the cafeteria to find out cabin and counsellor placements for the first of two week-long camp sessions.

"Heading Sycamore cabin will be Chris, Bailey and Abdullah!" shouts Jill.

As Jill continues the list of assignments, I realize we're the only trio of counsellors. Five pairs make up the rest.

Alright this will be easier, then.

Bailey is wheelchair-bound and there is one hella steep hill between one part of camp and the other. But one extra counsellor means more break times for each and less of a hassle organizing the six to eight campers we will get.

When we receive out camper files, we learn why we're grouped as a trio.

One camper, Michael, is apparently going through a rebellious phase, according to his file. Another camper, Lerman, is allergic to practically everything found in nature (and attending a camp smack dab in the middle of nature).

Another, Ralph, has high-functioning autism, ADHD and an auditory disorder. In a camp where order is imperative, he is chaos incarnate.

One camper, Dennis prefers arts and crafts to sports…and has some unspecified mood disorder. I really hope his disorder isn't too severe. Ralph seems hard enough. He can't be worse than Ralph.

The next morning, campers start to trickle in at ten thirty. Upon arrival, all families attend a small meet-and-greet with the medical team and cut their camper's insulin dose in half to adjust for the high-activity camp week ahead.

Staying on regular insulin levels would inevitably lead to low blood sugars during most activities. Heck, when I was a camper, the doctors reduced my insulin doses every single day—the entire medical team saw me as often as they saw each other.

Campers leave the medical team, set up their beds and then must part with their parents. Experienced families part ways easily. They know what camp is about and how safe it is.

Newer families, on the other hand, take some more persuasion.

Some campers are scared to leave their parents. In these cases, the parents usually help egg on their charge. Other campers, open to camp, have overprotective parents who micromanage their diabetics' health.

Mama used to be one. When your reality becomes constantly waking up throughout the night to make sure your child's blood sugar is under control and they aren't crashing into a coma, letting them sleep away from home seems like a ridiculous notion.

Before camp, I could never go on an overnight ski trip or a sleepover at a friend's house. I understand why now. But it didn't make the micromanaging and constant worry any less suffocating.

At eleven thirty, I run into my last camper.

"My name is Dennis." The introduction is short and polite. He's twelve, tall for his age, and very composed. He doesn't put up a fuss when he meets the doctors or when his head is checked for ticks.

"Hello, Dennis. I'm A-Abdullah. I'll be one of your three counsellors." *Stupid stutter stop showing up!* "You'll be in the Sycamore cabin. You can take your bags into that cabin at the far left."

"Alright."

I pull out a notepad from my cargo vest and cross his name off my list. That's all of them. When Dennis arrives at the cabin, he's the last of the eight campers to put his stuff down.

He sits down on his bunkbed with hands clasped in front of him and quietly watches Michael and Lerman run around popping the balloons and tearing down the streamers Chris, Bailey and I had painstakingly put up the night before.

He observes Kayleb and Seth jump on their beds. He smirks when he sees Kassian and Anthony run around playing tag, and at Ralph who tries and fails and tries again to join them in their mayhem.

He remains…calm. Composed.

"Hey, Abdullah!" Chris speed walks over to me soon after we enter the cafeteria for dinner.

"We're supposed to have eight campers!" he whisper-shouts, looking over his shoulder in the direction of the senior staff.

I pull out my notepad from my cargo vest, flip it open and read through the list of all the Sycamore campers. Michael and Lerman? Fooling around as usual. Seth? With Kayleb talking about ants or something. Kassian? Watching Anthony do some next Fortnite dance. Ralph? Looking at everything at once. Dennis?

"Where is Dennis?!" I sneak a glance at the senior staff. They seem occupied with the medical staff and haven't noticed our situation yet. "He might still be back in the cabin, I'll go—"

"Go, go! I'll keep watch with Bailey."

The longer it takes to find a camper the bigger the chance senior staff will find out and the bigger the chance that a covert camp-wide search will commence to clean up our mess. I sprint through the hallway to the Sycamore cabin and rush through the lounge to the washrooms. No feet stick out underneath any stalls. The back room is also empty. Which leaves…the bedroom closest to the entrance?

I enter the room and almost miss the brown cargo shorts and black shirt and puffy bloodshot eyes staring up at the ceiling from the top bunkbed.

"Dennis you…" I catch my breath. "You didn't come with the rest of the cabin for dinner. You okay?"

It's a dumb question but I don't know what else to say.

"No…" Dennis keeps staring at the ceiling. His eyes glisten. "I wanna go home…"

Damn it. Gonna be a drawn-out conversation. About FOMH—Feelings Of Missing Home—of all things.

Right before dinner!

Even worse—at a place like this! A counsellor alone with a camper is a big fat no. Without another witness, if events escalate, a camper's words will always veto the counsellor's.

"Hey, uh, I understand how you feel, but camp just started—"

"I want it to end!" Dennis bursts out. "I want…to die."

"Hey, um…" I try to find the right words. I'm not good with words on a normal day. "I know camp seems long, but it isn't gonna be that bad, and before you know it, camp will be finished and you'll barely have noticed!"

He stays in his bed. Tears crawl down his neck.

"Hey how about this, Dennis? If you miss your mom and dad—"

"What did you say?" Dennis snarls.

Shit! What did I mess up now?

"If you miss your…family…" I try. No reaction. Good. "You can write letters back home, give them to us and we can speed mail them through for you if that helps. But for that to happen, you need to come to dinner and then later at night you can write before bed."

I keep my distance. Dennis' expression remains unchanged. Then his snarl straightens. He wipes his eyes clean and gets up off his bed.

"Alright."

"Griffin! Can you watch my cabin for a bit! Thanks!" I briefly acknowledge Griffin's nod as I bolt past him out the hallway through the automatic doors and down the gravel path after Dennis.

The seven thirty morning summer sun shines the last bits of sleep out of my eyes and the cool breeze runs through my bed head and the rough gravel pavement rushes up to meet my bare and bruised feet. I forgot my shoes in the cabin.

Ya Allah (Oh God), all I want is one calm morning where nothing goes extremely wrong and I don't have to nonchalantly run after a—ow—camper. Ameeeeeeeeen.

The morning sounds like something out of a movie. One moment I'm trying to get my campers out of bed—and Michael and Lerman being Michael and Lerman decide to deliberately not get up.

Five seconds later, I'm down one camper who, previously motionless, jumps off his bunk, runs out the door, bolts through the lounge, exits the cabin and hobbles into the open air.

All of this in the time it takes me to step three metres away from Dennis to attend to Michael after waking him up and letting him calm down from whatever he was crying about through the night.

Damn it. I should've paid more attention to the bloodshot eyes.

"Dennis!" I yell at the twelve-year-old running and crying through the field. "Please stop!"

He doesn't.

He keeps running. Limping.

"Dennis! Why are you running? Where are you running to?"

"I'm going home! I hate this camp. Fuck you and fuck everyone and fuck this stupid camp. I want to go home!" yells the imploding diabetic. "I want to die."

He runs up the huge hill, past the recreation hall and towards the outdoor pavilion near the edge of camp. How do I stop him? A counsellor cannot touch another camper without consent. And no one would consent to being grabbed or restrained, least of all Dennis.

I don't know what exactly I could be convicted of. I just know it wouldn't be good.

Dr. Victoria happens to be nearby and spots us limping along. She walks over slightly behind me.

"You need any help?" she mouths over to me.

I think it over for a second. I don't even know what to do. I don't know how she can help me outside of being a witness and reporting every single mistake I will make to Griffin and Jackie and Jill. I shake my head no.

I try to look confident, as if I have a plan, as if I have dealt with this kind of situation before. Like I have a manual on what to do when a bipolar camper decides to run off in the early morning barefoot in some wack attempt to run out of camp all the way back home.

I think up of a possible delay and run over in front of my hobbling charge. I stand a few feet away from him and hold out my arms.

"Dennis, please stop!" I keep his gaze. "You know you can't actually run out of camp? You'll exhaust yourself before…"

Tears start to pour out of him. He tries to get past me. I shift back a bit, readjust myself in front of him and I try again. The dry pavement gives way to soft grass. My feet relax.

"Dennis, I know you miss your…" I remember not to say "Dad." Jill told us after our first dinner that Dennis has some family issues where "Dad" is essentially a trigger word for a bomb. "Your Mom a lot but look at it this way. It's already Tuesday. Today we have many fun activities, like Fire V.S. Ice, where the entire camp splits up and plays Capture the Pump—"

"I don't like sports too much." He's stopped advancing. Good.

"Uh, well in that case, there are still other activities you can enjoy throughout the day, like… art!"

A small smile peeks through his face.

"And tomorrow we will have a talent show. You have anything you wanna showcase for the talent show?"

"I can't think of anything right now."

"Well, don't worry, if you think of something, you can tell me later. And if you don't have something, you can always watch others. I've seen the talent show many times. It's amazing!"

A bigger smile.

"There's also swimming if you like that." I'm hoping his camper file is accurate.

"I do like swimming…"

Thank God.

"And if you still miss your mom, you can write her a letter every day, and we can email it to her for you. Did you try writing to her yet?"

"No. I guess not."

"But you can only do this"—I pause, both for dramatic effect, and to catch my breath—"if you stay and have fun at camp for only *three and a half more days*. It might seem long, but it will pass by faster than you know it, and you can tell your mom how much you enjoyed camp when you get picked up on Friday!"

"Alright." Dennis sniffles and begins to wince through the pain his body is starting to register. His adrenaline's drained out. He looks at his feet. He looks at my feet. His sniffles grow louder. Oh no.

"Dennis you alright, buddy?"

"I want to die."

He looks up, crying, his gaze unfocused towards the clear morning sky.

"Dennis, why do you keep saying that?"

"I cause others pain! I cry and yell and throw fits and others have to deal with it and I cause them pain and something is wrong with me and I want to die to cause no more pain."

"Dennis, hey, I would rather you express if something is wrong and we can help. Expressing yourself is healthy. Exploding, however, isn't."

I understand now why I should follow my own advice. I do not want to break down like Dennis.

"Come on. Let's get back to the cabin and see if you can't enjoy yourself."

I slowly start walking back to camp. Dennis follows. It's only eight in the morning and I'm exhausted.

"What are you drawing, Dennis?"

It's Thursday afternoon in the arts and crafts centre and, as opposed to Sunday, Monday and Tuesday morning, the rest of the session has gone by without too many problems. Michael and Lerman calmed down. Anthony, Kayleb, Seth, Kassian and Dennis enjoyed the last few days.

Ralph…remains chaotic. Some of the senior staff help us with him from time to time. Between Chris, Bailey and I, we're betting on how long it takes Ralph to get picked up tomorrow afternoon when everyone goes home.

"He's one of my own creations," Dennis beams. I glance down at the paper. A slasher smile positioned below two hollow circles in a floating face smiles back. The face floats on top of a misshapen body. Angel wings extend out of the back. "I'm gonna call him Trippity!"

I smile back. I used to draw something similar this past year. Not with a full body, but with slasher smiles and angry eyes, stitched teeth and burning eyebrows. I used to draw my own Trippity.

"Good job, Dennis. You can take that home with you tomorrow and show it to your mom."

"I have those at home!" Dennis points down at my shoes as we sit on the picnic benches outside. It's the farewell barbeque. Parents arrive. Soon they will sign out their kids and trickle away from the camp for the year.

Dennis points not at my shoes but at the Zubits on them—magnetic shoe closures which weave through laces and remove the need for tying.

"No way, really?" They're a Kickstarter. No one seems to know about them. Dennis is the first person in the year since I've worn them who recognized them.

"Yeah, I can't remember what they're called though." His eyebrows furrow in concentration.

"Zubits! That's great! I haven't met anyone else with them yet!"

"I'll show them next time I come!"

I hope I heard him correctly.

"That would be awesome! So, does that mean you'll come to camp again?"

"Yeah, it was…better than I expected."

He pauses to adjust his black cap and then looks up again.

"Thank you."

Chapter 25

Attention

It's eleven at night on Monday, August 13, 2018, and somehow the day is finally coming to an end. I sit outside the Sycamore cabin with Kassian trying to get through my batch of Camper Wellness Logs. Kassian is my last camper.

"Lerman! Michael! Stop running around. It's past eleven!" Chris yells from the cabin lounge. "Ralph! Have you brushed your teeth yet, buddy? No? Do it, please."

"Seth! Stop teasing Kayleb and let him sleep!" Bailey shouts from somewhere inside the cabin chaos. I don't look forward to dealing with it. Not that night cabin chaos is new. I remember when I was a Discovery camper and the first few nights were always the most trouble.

A few good campers try to fall asleep. A few get a taste of parent-free nights and go wild. A few taste parent-free nights and miss goodnight kisses. Everyone experiences an eleven p.m. curfew for the first time. No one gets much sleep.

I focus back on my Camper Wellness Log. I shift around on my portable three-legged stool. Kassian sits on a larger chair in front of me.

"Any aches, scrapes, bruises or pain?"

He scans his elbows and his knees and he shakes his head. "No."

"Alright, how're your eyes?"

"Good."

Kassian rubs his ears and then gives them the okay.

"Any mosquito bites?"

He checks. "Nope!"

I smile. Wellness logs are the one part of camp I didn't know existed until last year, my last time as a camper, which is strange considering I had been a camper for the three summers previously.

"Can you do a quick tick check for me?"

In a tree-filled grassy environment, a tick can hitch the hairline, latch onto a leg or drop down from a tree unnoticed.

Kassian ruffles his hands through his bright blonde hair and below his neck, then by his elbows and below his knees, and finally around his socks and under his chin. He finds none.

"Did you take..." A thundering armada of footsteps that make up the Pine cabin campers, the oldest female cabin opposite Sycamore, lumber past us, their counsellor, Kaitlyn, in the rear.

"Folks! Be quiet!" she yells. "Campers are sleeping!"

Kaitlyn notices us sitting outside. I raise two fingers to my forehead and give her a salute. It comes natural to me, my personal greeting. I smile wearily. Kaitlyn nods in acknowledgment, her smile apparent for a second, and then she focuses back on her loud campers.

Kassian and I stay silent until the campers pass. The wellness logs are confidential. They are kept as a record and known only to relevant staff members.

"Did you take a shower today?"

"Yes."

"Did you brush your teeth?"

"Yes."

"Did you pee and poo today?" I say as nonchalantly as possible.

He nods. Good. Hygiene is always important and with Wellness Logs, counsellors can keep track of when a camper took a shower or used the washroom. If a camper goes too long without doing any one of these, they can know and take appropriate measures.

"What was the highlight of your—"

"Abdullah, buddy, can you hurry up?" Chris yells from inside the cabin.

"Yeah, sure mate. We'll be right along in two minutes!"

I hate rushing wellness logs. I recall last year my counsellor, Benji, would take me to a picnic bench outside my cabin for my own Wellness Log check, under a pitch-black sky with a dim lamplight. In his Scottish accent he would ask if I had "any aches, scrapes or pains" and I would detail the story of every bruise or mosquito bite I could find. He would ask me what my favourite part of the day was and I would tell him not just my favourite part but my whole day.

"You don't have to tell me your entire day, you know," he once told me. "But I do enjoy it. You have very entertaining stories."

I turn my focus back on Kassian. "What was the highlight of your day?"

"I think…it would have to be high ropes!" Kassian beams the innocent eight-year old smile I wish I still had. I smirk back.

"And finally, on a scale from one to ten, how would you rate your day?"

"Ten out of ten!"

God, I wish all my campers were like Kassian!

"Abdullah!?" Chris yells again.

"Yeah, coming! Go on, Kassian. I'll follow."

I pick up my folder of wellness logs and my stool and go back inside to the unravelling Sycamore cabin.

Kayleb, Anthony, Kassian, Seth and Dennis are in bed. The only campers remaining are Ralph, Michael and Lerman.

"Alright, folks! Folks! Michael! Ralph! Lerman!" I shout. I get Michael and Lerman to stop for a second. Ralph follows suit. "If you don't get to sleep soon, I'll have to call Jackie…"

Michael and Lerman freeze.

"N-no, it's alright," Michael sputters.

"We'll go to bed right away," Lerman says as he rushes over to his bed. Ralph follows.

"That wasn't the most effective way to deal with the situation, folks…"

Jill's voice surprises me. I didn't realize she was right behind me. The senior staff member signals for us to follow her out of the cabin. I gulp and step out.

Bailey, Chris and I stand in front of Jill. At about five feet tall, Jill is shorter than Chris and me, but it's Chris who's shuffles side to side and me who constantly plays with my burn bracelet like a fidget spinner.

"Are all of your campers asleep?" Jill asks.

"Yes, they are!" Bailey answers for us.

Hopefully Lerman, Michael and Seth are asleep. God, they just seem to love to do whatever they're told not to do. Check your blood sugar? Nope. Stop running! Nah, let's have a race. Be quiet, please! How about we scream as loudly as possible instead.

One and a half days since camp started and Sycamore cabin is already known as being the late cabin, the messy cabin, the most chaotic cabin.

"Alright, just wanted to check in with you three. I know it's been a long day. How are things going with your campers?" Jill keeps a neutral face but her eyebrows furrow.

Attention

"The campers are alright. We have a few issues dealing with some, like Ralph," Chris responds. "But we should be getting things in order by tomorrow."

I nod in agreement. The situation is a bit more severe than that. But Jill will be evaluating us. No need to let her know how bad the situation might become.

"Alright. I'll be watching you folks to see if that's true. If you need help, feel free to ask me or Jackie or any of the senior staff."

She gives us each a pointed look.

"We will," I say and stand rigid until Jill leaves.

After she leaves, I check the hallway, close the door quietly and get ready for the impromptu Sycamore counsellor meeting.

"We gotta step up our game, a lot!" Chris begins.

My body feels heavy and my head nods forward as Chris lists the things we need to work better on. We plan until midnight. Our campers will be dressed and ready for activities thirty minutes before activities begin and in attendance fifteen minutes before they start.

Leaving fifteen minutes early gives just enough time to drag rebellious campers like Michael and Lerman and accounts for last-minute trips to the washroom (the entire Sycamore cabin at times). Most important, we'll communicate effectively with each other and remain in sync.

The next morning nullifies the entire night's worth of planning. Dennis runs away from camp. I run after him barefoot. With one less counsellor, one of the senior staff, the passing Griffin, steps in for a while, but even then, amid the chaos, order and precision remain forgotten. Chris, Bailey and I make sure Dennis feels alright and, in doing so, we pay less attention to Micahel and Lerman and Ralph and everyone else.

The chaos intensifies.

By lunch time, instead of chilling on the front yard waiting to be called to the cafeteria, the Sycamore cabin is a wreck, as if there had never been an hour-long meeting the night before.

"Michael! Lerman! Seth!" Bailey calls out, his wheelchair blocking one doorway. "Stop playing president. Please put down your cards and get ready for lunch!"

No one listens. It's like déjà vu.

Chris speed walks into the room through another entrance. Michael and Lerman lead the game of president, drawing in Seth, Kayleb and Anthony. Kiassian and Dennis watch from the sidelines while Ralph keeps running around the entire cabin.

"Michael, buddy, please get up, we need to make our way down to the cafeteria for lunch!" Chris' voice begins to rise. Michael ignores him. "Michael!" Chris repeats.

"Yeah, we'll get to it in a minute," Michael says and continues to look at his cards. Lerman throws down four Aces.

"Ha! Bet you can't beat that, Michael!"

"Oh, no?" Michael's face becomes smug as he throws down his second last card, a Joker, followed by his low three of clubs.

"What!? Nooooo!"

"Abdullah," I hear Jill's voice behind me. "A problem going on with your folks?"

"Uh..." Damn, how does she keep creeping up on me?

"Hey, Sycamore," Jill says and walks past me into the house of madness.

Well...shit.

"What are you folks playing?" Jill asks.

She stands five feet tall, almost even with Mitch.

"It's president," Michael replies and scrunches his face.

"Mind if I join?"

"Uh, sure. Alright then."

Michael collects the hands, shuffles and deals out the cards again, including to Jill.

What? Why is Jill playing with them at a time like this? We need to be at the cafeteria in ten minutes! Damn it! We are gonna be so late now, and on top of that, Jill will know exactly how dysfunctional the Sycamore cabin is if she didn't have a clear picture before.

"Damn Jill, you're really good!" Michael exclaims. "One game in and you're already president!"

"Thank you, Michael. I've just had a lot of practice with this before."

"Now I know you have to be dethroned!" Lerman laughs and starts to collect the cards to deal out the hands again.

"Actually folks, how about we set a rain check for the rematch? It's really close to lunch time and I hear the kitchen staff cooked something amazing!"

"Alright!" Mitch says and smiles.

Everyone rises up, reaches for their glucometers and hats and follows Jill out the door without complaint.

I stare blankly. What just happened?

Chapter 26

Miscellaneous Problems of the Food Kind

Ranch

When I arrived as a camper at Camp Discovery for the first time, it was the summer before grade nine. Back then, I knew two things about food.

One, I am Muslim, and I can only eat halal meat and that means it has been cut according to Islamic law, and some meat like pork is forbidden altogether. Two, the meat in quaint, rural London, Ontario, is anything but halal.

When I came back home after my five-day camp experience and Mama asked me about what I ate for dinner, I told her "Ranch on Pita" or "Ranch on Bread" or "Plain Ranch and Water."

"But *why?*" she had asked.

I said they were the only appetizing food on the menu. When she pointed out there were vegetarian options, I reiterated that I ate only the appetizing food on the menu.

Bags

"What is that?" Quinn points out as soon as we enter the dining hall for the first lunch of the second week-long camp session. This session I'm partnered with Alex, who Huronda ejected into Disco alongside another counsellor, Blaire.

"The higher ups didn't say it out loud," he said when we first became partners earlier in the week. "But the senior staff basically told Blaire and me at the end of C session that we could either come to Disco because y'all are short-staffed or we could pack our bags and go home early and skip out on D-sesh."

He frowned. I frowned.

I hope Discovery doesn't die off any time soon because of the short-staff situation. It already happened with an Ontario diabetes camp in Ottawa, Camp Banting.

I'm a counsellor at Sycamore again. Alex joins me as a pair to a group of six instead of eight campers. Chris became a counsellor for Samara, the youngest male cabin, while Bailey acts as a floater between multiple cabins.

"What's what, Quinn?" I ask.

He points to the milk.

"Why is it in a bag?"

"It's... always in a bag," Alex says and matches my confusion.

"It's a bag!" Quinn insists like it's the most obvious thing in the world. "With milk! Who does that?"

Why is Quinn acting like that?

Then I remember. Quinn just moved from Newfoundland.

They don't have bags of milk there.

Siesta

"Alright! I'm 4.6! Just a little bit more and I'll be there!" Carson rushes out of the cabin and into the yard, leaving his blood glucometer on the table. The disposable finger poker and strip remain undisposed.

"Carson, what are you doing?" I shout after our youngest camper.

It's just after lunch, 1 p.m., and that means it's time for the daily siesta, the Disco equivalent to the Huronda ZAP—an hour for campers and counsellors to rest after having been up and moving for the past five and a half hours.

Between breakfast and lunch, campers go through two activities of their choice. Some attempt the high ropes course. Others shoot arrows at archery. Some coop themselves in the arts and crafts centre, while others chill by the treehouse at the edge of camp. Still others play soccer or Frisbee or even wheelchair basketball up in the gym.

For campers between the ages of six and twelve years old, that should be enough activity for five and a half hours—right?

The Sycamore cabin seems to be the exception, whether it's last week's group of Dennis, Ralph, Michael and Lerman or this week's group of Brody, Carson and Quinn.

"My blood sugar is 4.6!" Carson resumes his mini-marathon.

"Wait, shouldn't you *not* run, then?"

"I'm running so that I'll get low and then I'll get to eat some dex!"

Low blood sugar means the glucose concentration in your blood dips below 4.0 millimolar. At that point, the body cannot produce enough energy, which can lead to muscle weakness, fatigue, dizziness and in severe instances, seizures and comas, and in the worst-case scenario, death. The one upside is that the treatment for such a condition is sugar and sweets. At camp, the sugar of choice is in small cylindrical flavoured tablets of dextrose—dex for short.

"Have you never had dex before?" I ask him.

I don't know how long Carson's been a diabetic but come on—eating Dex is, like, a universal diabetic experience.

"I've never had them. My mom says I've never gone low before," he says.

I blink.

"Carson! Buddy! You don't want to go low, trust me! I'm always low at camp and it sucks!" I say.

Damn it! I should stop Carson, right? But then...how? I can't touch him or push him! How do I make him stop running and not go low? Would it be better to just allow him to go low once and then bring him to the medical team?

"Yes! 4.1! Just a little bit more and I can eat dex!" Carson squeals as if he just saw a candy store.

Damn it! What should I do?

Carson checks his blood sugar two minutes later. "No! Darn it! It's 5.1 now." He groans and walk back to the cabin looking defeated. "I'll never get to eat dex..."

My shoulders relax as I follow him back inside.

How the world will come to an end

Many theories abound about how the world will end. Some people postulate dust storms or asteroids or a global plague or something grand as a result of humanity's neglect of nature.

I have a different theory.

On the first Thursday of camp and the last full day of the first session, Kayleb approaches me as we slowly make our way to the gym for a talent show.

Kayleb remains one of the calmer, easier-to-deal-with campers of Sycamore. He seems to enjoy camp, doesn't cause trouble and he's never a headache—

"Hey Abdullah, wanna see me eat a leaf?" Kayleb asks with a completely serious face.

"What? Kayleb, no! Why? No. Just, no! Don't…"

Kayleb ignores me and walks up to a small nearby tree, plucks a leaf and munches on it as if it were candy for the rest of the way to the gym.

Exactly one week later, at the second closing campfire, after having got rid of his dex addiction by experiencing how bad it feels to go low, instead of telling either Alex or me that he is still hungry after snack, Carson picks a twig off the ground and starts chewing it.

I tell him to stop the first time. I give him my emergency snack bar when I see him chewing through the same stick like a beaver five minutes later.

Thus, the world will come to an end when it's overrun by multiple Kaylebs and Carsons who, all of a sudden, start to chew through bark and eat through leaves and leave nothing left to produce the oxygen we need to breathe.

I want dex!

One constant among Sycamore boys seems to be an excessive amount of energy. It was Ralph in the first camp session. Then it was Carson running to go low and wanting to eat dex. Now it's Quinn and Brody, my oldest and youngest campers, running around after evening snack at eight thirty trying to go low once again.

The setting sun streaks orange-pink colours through the trees that surround the camp. After evening snack, campers should be off to bed.

Yet Quinn and Brody run rampant in and out of the cafeteria, around the totem pole outside and over and under some picnic tables.

I suck in a deep breath. I pinch the bridge of my nose. Quinn and Brody are in not in danger of going low yet, they just had banana bread, and can probably jog for another hour. I can't convince them through their health. Maybe Quinn might listen? He seems relatively well-mannered.

"Quinn, please stop!" I shout.

"Yeah, we will. Just a second!"

"You need to give them attention. Campers won't say it out loud but they don't have their parents to impress, the only ones looking after them is you. If they can impress you or hold your attention, they will feel happy and listen to you."

Jill's words from last week reach back to me. She was advising Chris, Bailey and me after we asked her how she managed so easily to gain Michael's attention.

Alright, then.

"Quinn! Brody! Wanna race?"

Quinn stops. Brody looks up and his face morphs from startled to pleasantly surprised in an instant.

"Alright!"

"Let's go!"

"Alex," I turn around to my co-counsellor who watches on amused. "You mind starting us off?"

"Yeah sure, man." He walks over to a tent canopy and points to a pole. "Y'all can start from here. Run all the way to the gazebo." He points to a brown Japanese-style building ninety metres away. "Then run back."

Quinn, Brody and I line up by the pole. Quinn brushes back his shoulder-length, blonde, rock star hair and kneels ready to bolt.

Brody stands next to Quinn, his head reaching Quinn's shoulder, his face scrunched up as he focuses on the gazebo. He shifts his legs, glances at us to see we haven't left, glances back to the gazebo, then to Alex, and waits for the signal to bolt.

"Ready? Get set..."

Brody bolts.

"Brody! Not yet!" Brody stops two metres away and looks to Alex, who shakes his head and then backpedals back to his position.

"Ready? Get set. Go!"

I rush forward at full sprint. I keep low to the ground. I pull my hands back to my sides as if I was a ninja from Naruto.

"AAAAAHHHHH!!!" I yell and deafen everyone. My sight narrows in on the gazebo.

Gone are the picnic tables out on the yard. Gone are the medical staff and senior staff. Gone are the shrub-like trees by the edge of the grass. Gone are Quinn and Brody behind me, their soft thuds on the grass barely registered, and all that remains is me and the brown gazebo in the distance, erect in the twilight, catching the last bits of orange-pink dusk.

I slam into the railing and bounce in the opposite direction. Quinn, a few paces behind, and Brody, slightly further back, laugh throughout the run. My mouth tastes of metal. I don't run often. I don't yell often, either. I almost trip on the flat grass and catch myself. Quinn catches up.

The campers and counsellors come back into my peripheral. I keep yelling. I probably look like a lunatic. I wish someone was recording it. I swivel my head behind for a second. Quinn nears. He's fast for a fifth grader. Or I'm just slow.

I look back from the front and catch sight of the tent pole. It's thin, as wide as two fingers, and as flimsy as a blade of grass in the wind. I rush past Alex and push my legs further.

To go further, BEYOND!

The Dragon Ball meme runs through my head. I picture a deep ocean inside myself and pull, releasing an entire tsunami of hidden power. I pour it all into my legs and spring forward to reach the tent pole as if it was some miraculous trident of power I was racing towards and not just an ordinary piece of metal.

I win.

Barely.

I race past the pole and then stop with Quinn behind me. I heave in. I heave out.

"Woo…hoo!" I yell between shallow, metallic breaths. "That was awesome!"

"Oh-oh!" Brody shouts behind me. "Can we do it again?"

I pant, look over to Brody, and smile.

"Gonna have to take a rain check on that Brody. Maybe later. We need to head back to our cabin, alright?"

"Sure!"

Chapter 27

Broken Bones and Stitches

It's right before dinner at five o'clock on the Tuesday of the second session, rain drenches the field outside and all thirty-six campers surprisingly are not in the cafeteria as I expected, when I find myself on the receiving end of a fully-panicked co-counsellor.

"Alright, dude!" Alex shouts and power-walks over to me, his face tight and alert. "Can you tell me exactly what is going on? What the *hell* is going on with Carson?"

His eyes remain widened. He shifts his gaze to the incident form in my hand. His eyebrows shoot up. "Hold up, man, and tell me what do you know about him?" I try to calm him down but Alex blows up.

"All I've got is that one of my campers seems to be missing, possibly hospital-bound. If what Kaitlyn saw is correct, he has a bone sticking out of his leg and might need stitches in Emergency if what I overheard from Griffin is correct. And to top everything off, Griffin told me to just nonchalantly block an entire camp worth of eager and hungry tweens from entering what looks like an empty med cabin but is, actually, you know, a freaking operation theatre with my camper as the star of the show!"

He rubs his temples and looks at me expectantly.

"See," I say. "So what actually happened…"

I folded my prayer mat and tucked it into its bag. As a Muslim, I pray five times a day. I used to be nervous about bringing it up among people who knew nothing about Islam. After a few summers, I did start to pray at camp.

Everyone was and still is very accommodating. All I need are ten minutes alone every few hours and I can pray. It helps that, being so far away from home, I can offer a shortened prayer.

After I said my prayer, I rushed out of the empty Sycamore cabin. While the second batch of campers seemed easier to deal with than last session, I knew Alex could only hold down so many tweens on his own for so long.

When I reached the cafeteria, Sycamore was already seated—inside with everyone else until the medical staff called on them. It was pouring hard outside. I caught sight of Carson exiting the washroom by the cafeteria and walking—with a limp?—towards me.

"Abdullah, my ankle hurts. A lot!" he said as he touched the ground tenderly with his right foot. His wide blue eyes flinched at the pain.

"Um, can you still move your foot?"

"It hurts a lot!"

"There's a doctor in the med cabin." I kept my voice steady. "How about we go there and have them take a look, alright?"

I nudged him forward. I needed to tell Alex that I would be gone with Carson. Last camp session I didn't do that and it royally screwed my communication with my co-counsellors, Chris and Bailey. I scanned the dining hall and found the Sycamore table. Alex looked at me with his face scrunched in confusion.

"I'm taking Carson to the med cabin." I pointed to him and gestured with my hands in the general direction of the med cabin.

Dr. Robbie and Nurse Kendra were looking over the menu at their table and counting the carbs in each dish. A few nurses and student nurses prepared the rooms with insulin supplies. I spied one student nurse emptying out a sharps container into a large, bright yellow biohazard bin.

"Excuse me!" I stopped at the doorway with Carson. "His ankle hurts badly. Could you please take a look at it?"

Dr. Robbie took a moment to register Carson's pained expression and then pulled a chair up beside him. "Sure, Carson, can you please sit over here? Kendra, could you pull up one more chair in front of him? We need to prop up his foot."

I stayed behind the growing medical crowd. They pulled off Carson's sock and shoe. His ankle looked swollen, red and bulging.

"Carson, can you move your ankle?" Dr. Robbie asked.

"It hurts a lot!" He rotated the foot slowly.

Nurse Kendra placed a light hand on it to feel the bone. "Doesn't look like anything too major, but it could start to fester if we don't treat it. Emma, can you get a few alcohol swabs, a few band aids and medical tape, please?"

Dr. Robbie sat back for a moment and stared at the swollen appendage. "He might have a small hairline fracture, if anything, but that seems unlikely. Abdullah." He turned toward me. "What sort of activities did you do today?"

"Heroes and Villains today, sir. I don't know what everyone else did, but the counsellors were split off and organized games and obstacles for the campers. I built a laser maze in Bruce Power out of strings and tape."

"It's probable Carson twisted or overexerted himself in one of the challenges. Chances are it's just a swollen ankle from today's activities. Still, we shouldn't take any chances."

The doctor took out his walkie-talkie and found an open channel. "Dr. Robbie to any senior staff member. Dr. Robbie to any senior staff member." The command blurts out of my walkie-talkie as well.

"You need something, sir?" the camp director, Griffin, stepped in and announced. Strange. This isn't his first time coincidentally drifting past a sticky Sycamore situation. He had been right by the Sycamore cabin the day Dennis made a mad dash last camp session. I'm starting to think he has a sixth sense for Sycamore screw-ups-to-be.

"We got a camper here, Carson from Sycamore, and he seems to have twisted his ankle due to today's activities. It's nothing too major, but we want to get him to the hospital just to make sure."

Griffin's expression remained neutral and then his mouth formed a small 'Oh.'

"Alright, I'll inform senior staff and we'll get the ambulance ready."

"Griffin, one question?" I jumped in. He halted at the door. "This warrants an incident report, right?"

I knew the answer. I don't know why I asked.

"Yes you should probably get to work on that right away, Abdullah," he said and closed the door behind him.

"Oh, damn it!" Dr. Robbie said and sighed. "I forgot to tell Griffin we should call the hospital ahead of time and prepare emergency. They usually aren't too busy and we want Carson to be treated ASAP so he can get back to camp activities."

"Try radioing him," Kendra suggested. "He had his on him, I'm pretty sure."

"Right! Good save!" Dr. Robbie turned away and spoke into the walkie-talkie. "Med Staff to Griffin Moore. Med staff to Griffin Moore."

"You should go and write that incident report, Abdullah," Kendra noticed my still motionless form. "We've got things covered here."

Kendra motioned to the six medical staff huddling around Carso to clean his wound and apply a band aid.

"Oh, yeah, sure," I stared at Carson's right leg and started to think. He might have a small hairline fracture if what the doctors said is correct. His ankle, which looked bruised and possibly broken, perhaps due to the earlier strenuous activities that occurred during the day and is being treated right now at 5:46 p.m.

"Right bruised ankle, slightly swollen, possibly broken. Right bruised ankle, slightly swollen…" I repeated to myself as I walk out the hallway.

I never filled an incident report before—on the contrary, I've been the subject of an incident form when I almost drowned last summer on the first day of camp. I can't mess this up.

The hall brimmed with campers. I spotted a slight opening and quicken my normally slow pace. I slid left to avoid one camper. Shuffled back to not run into another. Made a right lunge and avoided a swarm of girls.

"Yo! Dude!" Alex seemed to teleport across my path. "What's…"

I twirled around him. "Sorry, I got a small incident report to fill out," I said and raced towards the now-empty dining hall.

Incident forms were supposed to be located on the corner table where senior staff sits. The table was littered with cut-up cardboard, open scissors, used tape rolls and squeezed-out glue bottles.

A small box with a blazing fire insignia and the words "Disco Inferno" emblazoned in red stood on the corner table. Campers and counsellors can write notes about some new achievement such as "put on an insertion site for the first time" or "did their own injection for the first time." Senior staff read them out during evening snack with each achievement followed by applause and one of three possible cheers.

When I was a camper, the box was also used to insert surprise pranks and challenges to campers. I tried pranking a cabin mate once to sing "I'm a little teapot." It backfired when senior staff made the entire Maple cabin sing "I'm a little tea pot" instead. I've never tried it again.

A mess of forms lay splattered on the other end of the round table opposite the Disco Inferno box. I rifled through them.

Where is it? Emergency form? Nope. Police telephone and other important numbers? Nope. Incident Form? No—wait, yes! I pulled out a pen from one of my many pockets. Let's see. Name? Carson. Age? Eight. Gender? Male. Incident? There was a long list of possible boxes I could check off.

Now.

Which categories includes "possibly-but-not-sure-if-camper-has-broken-bones-from-falling"?

Ah-ha! There it is…

"Alright, dude!" someone interrupted.

I looked up.

"And that's what we have so far!" I tell Alex. His face loses its panic, adrenaline and anger. Only shock and exhaustion still register.

"Wait, so Carson probably only has a twisted ankle? Not a bunch of broken bones and stitches?"

"Yup, that seems to be the case."

"I need a break, man," Alex drawls out.

"Wait a sec, if you're here, whose watching our cabin?"

Alex purses his lips and then, under his breath he lets out, "Fuck!"

Chapter 28

Alex

I ran into Alex for the first time during ZAP free time at Camp Huronda. I had to shadow the Beaver cabin counsellors, Kyle and Jamie, for the day before heading off to Discovery. Alex, their co-counsellor, was on break.

For the Beaver cabin, ZAP (Zero Activity Period) consists largely of campers reading books or magazines, sleeping or trying to sleep, or cleaning up their bedside table if Kyle deems it unclean. One or two campers seem antsy, eager to move and play around.

As soon as we reach the cabin after dinner, Jamie heads to his bed, kicks off his Birkenstocks, rolls himself up in his sleeping bag and crashes. Alex lies in a bed near Jamie. He lazily scans the cabin.

A few socks lay scattered by one bedside. A dusty guitar case stands on the other side. A few hats and a glucometer rest precariously on top. Multiple burn bracelets hang off his wrist, each commemorating a different year at camp. One catches my eye—a white, red and green one identical to mine.

Yet Alex wasn't a part of my LDP group like Jamie. I hadn't seen him last year as a counsellor, either. So, that means…Alex's eyes open.

"Sup. I'm Alex," he says and introduces himself. "Abdullah, you happen to be a part of the July LDPs from last year?"

"Actually, yeah. You noticed the burn bracelet?"

"Mhm. Benji and Megan gave us the same ones."

"Makes sense. Jamie has it as well."

Alex goes back to sleep. I don't see him for most of the next day. I don't think much more about him. I have to prepare for camp.

"Ah shit, man! Can you just end your turn already?" Gian Franco groans as I successfully invade and take Kamchatka from him. Flicking his troops off, I take some from Japan and put them on my new Risk territory.

"Nah, fam!" I grin and roll the dice again after declaring an attack on Chris' Siberia. I have six troops in Kamchatka to Chris' two. This should be an easy win. I roll my three attack die, he rolls his two defence die. I roll five, five and three to his six and four. One loss to each player. We are now five to one.

"Abdullah man, face it, you ain't getting through Siberia," Chris says and shoots a triumphant smile plastered on his face.

It's ten in the evening in London, Ontario. We reached Camp Woodeden a few hours ago. Griffin, the camp director, told us to take the day off and rest from the travel. We will know our cabin co-counsellors tomorrow when the entire staff team arrives and finish staff training. Five counsellors sit in the camp dining hall—Chris, Gian-Franco, Taite and Kaitlyn. Senior staff are up in the recreation centre on the hill.

"Do you guys need another plague?" Taite says. She gave up pretty early on in the game, but we decided to spice the game up by leaving her remaining pieces as neutral obstacles and allowing her to "plague" the game every so often and randomly kill off troops across the world.

"I say do it!" Kaitlyn, observing the game from a few tables away, injects her own opinion.

Alex

"Oh my God!" shouts a voice from down the hall.

Pause.

"Shit!"

Pause.

"Alright, I think this is the dining…" The sliding doors leading to the camp grounds open. "Ah, shit!"

Alex, dressed in a Blue-Jays shirt, shorts and camp hat, strolls into the dining hall dragging his sleeping bag. He looks around, takes in the round tables, chairs, refrigerators and closed kitchen, and then turns his gaze back to the sliding doors.

"Yo, there aren't any more automatic doors or some shit, are there?"

"Not in this building, but why is that a problem?" I ask.

"See, Blaire dropped me off and she went to park her car. At first I couldn't find anyone, but then I ran into Griffin, and he told me to come to this building. I reach here and as I reach out to open the door, the freaking door swings out and almost smashes my face!"

"Wait, you didn't know Disco had automatic doors?" I try to suppress a laugh but my mouth curls up.

"How was I supposed to know? Then, I'm coming down the hallway and all these cabin rooms are to my left. They seem much better than the ones at Huronda, by the way."

"Yeah, Disco is like a hotel or resort compared to Huronda."

"You don't say? Anyway, so I'm looking into one of the rooms through a window, and I'm walking, when bam! This one door randomly just swings open five feet away from me! And there isn't anyone there again!"

"Duh, they're automatic."

"Dude, I know, but, like, you sure this camp isn't haunted by ghosts or some shit?"

Compasses are used in most contexts to navigate ships or orient maps or find your way back home. In most cases, it's a physical device. In the case of the 2017 LDPs at Huronda, "Compass" by Lady Antebellum becomes our anthem. It has a tempo that undoubtedly pulls every LDP back in time to that one glorious summer.

It's no wonder, then, that when I approach Alex and Blaire with the idea of playing Compass at the talent show on the last night of the first camp session, they have the same idea.

It's also no wonder, then, that when we do play in the dry gym on a rainy Thursday, it's a failure. Barely anyone can hear our dismal voices amid the echoing gym acoustics. I can't sing for shit and even if they could hear me or I could sing, the song's depth would remain lost to all non-LDPs. Lost to everyone but the three of us.

The most tedious part of camp is probably the paperwork. It isn't the hardest. Dealing with homesick campers is more difficult. It is, however, one of the last things that must to be done before the session ends. Each group of counsellors is obligated to fill out a bunch of questions about a camper, and comment on observations and findings that future counsellors might find useful.

I fill out a form on camper Brody during my hour break on a Thursday afternoon. Most breaks I usually rest in the staff lounge away from campers. Today, I sit at the empty table in the cabin lounge. It's two in the afternoon and the rest of the cabin has gone swimming. My prayer mat lies next to me and my rain jacket slopped in a pile in front of me. A walkie-talkie blares loudly nearby. I barely notice. My eyelids feel like weights. I drag my pen through the form.

Alex

I love camp. I truly do. I love jumping on high ropes and playing Risk and smashing logs to smithereens on wilderness trips and racing against campers while yelling like a lunatic. But I also love sleeping until noon and not waking up at seven thirty in the morning.

I put my cheek against my left hand and prop up my head with my prayer mat like a pillow. I keep writing with my right hand.

"Any details you would like future counsellors to know?" the form reads out.

"Likes to run for Dex," I write and scribble out. I try to keep my writing as neat as possible. Future counsellors probably won't like an illegible mess. I keep writing. And writing. And writing…

"Yo, bro! Might wanna wake up!" Alex shouts at me.

I open my eyes and look up. My pen remains poised in my hand in mid-stroke. My cheek hurts from where it lay on my knuckles. My neck feels stiff. I blink rapidly and squeeze the sleep out. I glance around the cabin. The walkie-talkie remains on full blast. It seems Sycamore cabin has returned and how long ago I don't know.

"Did…did I doze off?"

"More like went into hibernation." Alex grins. His phone remains half-hidden behind his back. "The walkie-talkie has been blasting full volume for God knows how long. You seemed dead to the world, mate."

In my life, few things outside my family remain constant. I drifted through nine schools, two countries and three cities. Many things changed over the years.

But one of the few constants years is my diabetes. I'm diabetic and have been for nine years and will probably remain a diabetic until death do us part. Procrastination seems to be the other constant in my life.

It's eleven thirty at night on the last Thursday of the last session. The campers sleep while Alex and I finish paperwork. More specifically, the camper awards. Crisp and blank, certificates lie in a pile on the lounge table ready to give a title to a specific camper based on something Alex and I decide to highlight.

"Alright, first one we got is…Cody." Alex pulls a certificate off the top. "Cody Bell is awarded as the camper most likely to…."

He stares at the paper. I stare at the paper.

"Let's come back to this one," I say and place the certificate at the bottom of the pile.

"Let's see." Alex pulls the next one. "Jonathan."

"That's easy. Camper most likely to become the next Houdini!" I laugh. Jonathan showed magic card tricks and performed as a magician during the talent show. Houdini was definitely a few more card tricks down the line.

"Alright and then…Carson?"

"Most likely to…eat a stick?" I suggest and immediately take it back. That can't be considered an achievement.

"Most likely to…oh, how about Not Go Low?" Alex suggests.

I agree. Carson, for all his complaints and innocent mischief, almost never went low…ever. Even back at home.

"And Brycen?" Alex asks.

Alex

I blank out. Brycen remained quiet and well-behaved throughout camp. He was Carson's older friend back home and the two acted like brothers. But compared to Carson, Brycen was just…a good camper.

"Let's skip him for now. We can do him after," I suggest.

"Now we got Brody."

I pull out the other eight-year-old's award-to-be. Easy. I look at Alex.

"Most likely to Run for Dex?" I say with a raised eyebrow.

"Definitely," Alex agrees and snorts a chuckle. "Most likely to Run for Dex."

Brody had become almost philosophical earlier. For the last activity of the final night, campers and counsellors are allowed to stay up slightly past the ten thirty curfew and do a planned, calm, final activity.

Alex and I had decided to take them up the hill near the Bruce Power Complex to lie down on some big wooden boxes and stargaze. The view wasn't as good as when Alex and I did it on our LDP wilderness trip in Algonquin Park, but it sufficed…until Brody started asking questions about the universe and higher beings that put me in a low panic.

These topics come with opinions and, if not handled properly, they can lead to campers being influenced by counsellors. The last thing I wanted was to be called in and questioned about why Brody suddenly became Muslim.

"Now we got Quinn," Alex said.

Another easy one.

"Definitely most likely to become a rock star."

Quinn has shoulder-length blonde hair and blue eyes and already plays the guitar and is a walking encyclopedia at camp regarding anything music-related.

"You know." Alex chuckles. "I wouldn't be surprised if in a few years he holds a concert and we run into him there."

"Yeah man, we can say we were the ones who set him down this path with this superb award."

I motion toward the printed piece of paper.

"And that brings us back to...Cody."

Alex pauses. I pause.

"Cody...most likely to...uh...Alex, you got any ideas?"

"Nah. You?"

"Nah."

Cody Bell is perhaps one of the most average campers at camp. He's a grade five graduate, polite and slightly insecure when it comes to his guitar skills, although comparing oneself to Quinn is not a good idea. He's quiet but also really excited by most activities. He isn't Kassian, who had a ten out of ten almost every day, but he isn't Dennis, either, who went through a subtle transformative experience over the course of five days. Cody Bell is...average.

Same with Brycen.

And it's almost midnight! Ugh.

I get up from my seat and move towards the sink in the hallway outside the staff washroom. Above are numerous cabinets once half-filled with medical supplies. Now, at the end of the camp, all that remains are a couple bottles of Glucerna, a milkshake advertised as a full meal replacement and used as an emergency drink to stabilize blood sugars after having four tablets of Dex and waiting for fifteen minutes.

Glucerna comes in chocolate, strawberry, wild berry and best of all, vanilla. Glucerna is the drink Alex and I have toasted with for every night this past week, low blood sugar or not.

Alex

I grab two vanillas and plump down on the sofa chairs by the walls. Alex drags himself over next to me. I wordlessly pass him his bottle. This is our nightly routine. Tonight is the last night.

Crik! Crik! Pop!

The muted bottle caps twist open and the vanilla aroma wafts to our noses. We both lean back, take a deep breathe, and exhale.

"To ketones!" Alex says. We toast and sip.

"To broken bones and stitches!" I shout another toast. Alex guffaws.

"To eating sticks and leaves!" Alex chortles. I try and keep my laughter down.

"To running for Dex!" I say and look down at my worn-out shoes.

I wonder what the campers would think if they saw us right now.

"To a job well done, mate!"

Alex grins.

I lean back into the sofa. The night nurses are probably making their rounds right about now to check the campers' blood sugars. They've seen us up multiple times before. They don't mind.

"To diabetes, man, without which we never would have met," I utter like a person of higher society.

I look into my bottle. The Glucerna's almost gone. We make a last toast and chug down our drinks. I jerk my head towards the cabinet again. Alex nods.

Another Glucerna it is.

Acknowledgements

I don't need to say much more about myself that you, the reader, doesn't already know.

The relevant bits at least.

I do, however, want to acknowledge that this book could not have come about without the help of multiple people.

I thank my parents for moving to Canada and staying in Canada after my diagnosis. Thanks to them I gained the experiences and confidence needed to talk about diabetes.

I thank my copyeditor, John Dunford, and my cover designer, Hafsa Siddiqui and my content editors Hafsa Ahmed, Erub Khan and Alexis Whelan. This book would be nowhere near as polished without their help.

Finally, I thank Professor Guy Allen and instructors Rahul Sethi, Laurel Waterman, John Currie, and Robert Price at the University of Toronto Mississauga, as well as Mr. Michael Morano and Dr. Jaroslaw Szecowka at St. Francis Xavier Secondary School, without whose classes I could never have gained the skills, passion, pressure or initiative to write these stories.

www.ingramcontent.com/pod-product-compliance
Lightning Source LLC
Chambersburg PA
CBHW042056290426
44112CB00001B/3